ANTILLEAN SEASHELLS

Hendrik Elingsz van Rijgersma, at the age of 38. (The original picture was made in October 1873 by photographer A. Greiner in Amsterdam.)

ANTILLEAN SEASHELLS

*the 19th century watercolours
of caribbean molluscs
painted by
Hendrik van Rijgersma*

BY

HENRY E. COOMANS

DE WALBURG PERS

Dedicated to ROGER and SAMIA MARTIN
malacologists and shell collectors in
the West Indies and on the Philippines
ardent students of the Conidae
honorary assistent at the American Museum
of Natural History in New York (1960-1965)
awarded with the Medal 'Natura Peperit Scientiam'
of the Zoological Museum Amsterdam (1988)

and sincere friends of

THE AUTHOR

Published with financial aid of the
'Overlegorgaan Kulturele Samenwerking Nederlandse Antillen'
(OKSNA), Curaçao

© 1989 Henry E. Coomans, Bloemendaal (Holland)

Niets uit deze uitgave mag worden verveelvoudigd en/of openbaar gemaakt door middel van druk, fotokopie, microfilm of op welke andere wijze ook zonder voorafgaande schriftelijke toestemming van de uitgever.

No part of this book may be reproduced in any form, by print, photoprint, microfilm or any other means, without written permission from the publisher.

CIP/ISBN 906011.616.X

FOREWORD

Shells and shellfish have been of great importance to the original population of the Antillean Islands. The Indians used the animals for food, whereas the shells were manufactured into tools or weapons, and the colourful ones served as ornaments.

When the first European explorers visited the West Indies, the beautiful shells were taken home and placed in 'cabinets of curiosities'. In later years shell collectors gathered them on the beaches, not only for pleasure but also for scientific purposes.

The island of St. Martin seemed to be famous for its shell fauna, as we can read in M. D. Teenstra's book 'De Nederlandsche West-Indische Eilanden in derzelver tegenwoordigen toestand'. In 1837 he wrote: 'The bays of this island are rich in fish but nothing exceeds the beauty and variety of the multitude in shell species, which are found on the beaches'.

Therefore, it does not surprise us that the Dutch physician H. E. van Rijgersma, who was interested in animals and plants, assembled a large collection of shells when he lived on St. Martin from 1863 to 1877. In addition he collected on some other islands of the Caribbean. During the year 1875 he described these shells in a manuscript, illustrated by himself with eighty beautiful watercolours. Unfortunately doctor Van Rijgersma was not able to finish the manuscript due to his death in 1877. It took almost one century before his manuscript and another one about the plants of St. Martin were rediscovered in the United States. After the book 'Flowers from St. Martin' by Henry and Maritza Coomans, published last year by De Walburg Pers, we can enjoy now the attractive watercolours of 'Antillean Seashells' as they were painted by Hendrik van Rijgersma on St. Martin.

Biological science and artistic refinement are combined here by the author and publisher in a splendid work, which represents the first documentation on molluscs of the Netherlands Antilles.

Edsel A. V. Jesurun
Minister Plenipotentiary
of the Netherlands Antilles

The Hague, February 22, 1989

Fig. 1. *Coat of Arms of the Van Rijgersma family. (Drawing J. Zaagman.)*

CONTENTS

Foreword, by Minister E. A. V. Jesurun		5
Introduction, by Prof. Dr. L. B. Holthuis		9
Biography of Hendrik Elingsz van Rijgersma (1835-1877)		11
History of Malacological Research on the Netherlands Antilles		19
Van Rijgersma and Malacology		25
Shell Collection		25
Library		27
Contacts and Correspondence		28
Travels		33
References in Malacological Literature		33
Manuscript on Westindian Molluscs		35
Plates		37
Prosobranchia	Strombidae	38
	Cypraeidae	52
	Eratoidae	62
	Cassidae	68
	Tonnidae	82
	Bursidae	86
	Ovulidae	92
	Ranellidae (Cymatiidae)	96
	Colubrariidae	118
	Conidae	122
	Turridae	148
Opisthobranchia	Pleurobranchidae	152
Pulmonata	Ellobiidae	156
Pelecypoda	Cardiidae	164
	Verticordiidae	178
Scaphopoda	Dentaliidae	180
Literature		185
Index		189
Acknowledgements		192

Fig. 2. *St. Martin, Back street anno 1897. (Dr. Van Rijgersma had his office in this street.)*

INTRODUCTION

When starting my studies on the Decapod Crustacea of the Netherlands Antilles in 1956, I came across a short paper by T. H. Streets (1872) dealing with a collection of Crustacea from St. Martin made by a Dr. H. E. van Rijgersma. The Dutch name of the collector, of whom I had never heard before, awoke my interest in his person, which even increased when I found material collected by him still present in the collection of the Academy of Natural Sciences of Philadelphia. When I found in the archives of the Rijksmuseum van Natuurlijke Historie several letters from Van Rijgersma addressed to the entomologist of the Museum at that time, Dr. S. C. Snellen van Vollenhoven, I decided to try and find out more about Van Rijgersma, his life and his work.

I was most thrilled therefore when Dr. Henry E. Coomans with much ingenuity managed to unravel the entire history of Van Rijgersma's life, his family relations as well as his scientific contacts and other interesting information. Coomans furthermore managed to obtain many of the notes and documents left by Van Rijgersma, and to copy those items that could not be obtained. In Coomans' thesis all this information is now brought together and made available to the scientific public. The publication of Van Rijgersma's watercolours of plants (issued in 1988) and Molluscs (the subject of the present book) puts the crown on Dr. Coomans' efforts to make Van Rijgersma better known and to give him the recognition that he so fully deserves.

It is namely seldom realized, not even by scientists themselves, how much science owes to, often almost anonymous, workers in the field, who as a hobby (sometimes almost amounting to a calling) gather data on the subjects of their interest. The publication of such data, either by the collector himself or by other specialists dealing with the subject, can be of immense value to science. So far Van Rijgersma's contribution has been that he collected material which was studied and published by American, French and Dutch zoologists. As a collector, however, he was soon almost forgotten, most undeservedly so. But now, through the efforts by Dr. and Mrs. Maritza Coomans, Van Rijgersma's own work will be offered to the public. May it get the appreciation that it so richly deserves.

Prof. Dr. L. B. Holthuis

Leiden, 14 March 1989

GENEALOGICAL TREE OF THE VAN RIJGERSMA FAMILY
(for details and biographies see Coomans, 1974)

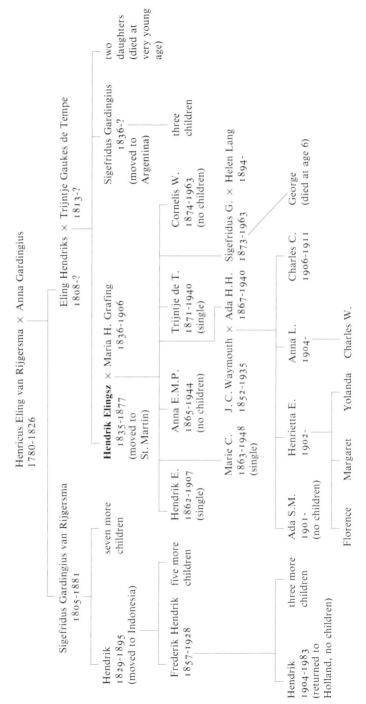

BIOGRAPHY OF HENDRIK ELINGSZ VAN RIJGERSMA
(1835-1877)

Hendrik van Rijgersma was born on 5 January 1835 in Lemmer, province of Friesland, the Netherlands. His father, Eling Hendriks, was pharmacist in this town, whereas his grandfather, Henricus Eling, had been minister of the Dutch Reformed Church in Cubaard. The Van Rijgersma family belongs to the old Frisian nobility with their own coat of arms (fig. 1). A genealogical tree is given on page 10.

Nothing is known about his childhood, but he must have had a good education, and it is supposed that he visited the 'Latijnse school' (Latin school). Het could speak a number of languages: next to Dutch also Frisian, being member of a real Frisian family and born in Friesland. For his later profession he needed Latin, and in correspondence he used English and French.

Hendrik wanted to become a physician, therefore he worked as an assistent with the physician of Oostzaan, a small town near Amsterdam. In the 19th century it was possible to study medicine at one of the Universities in the Netherlands, whereas a lower degree could be obtained after passing tests before the Provincial Medical Commission. Van Rijgersma passed both examinations for 'Heelmeester voor het platte land' (Physician for the countryside) and 'Vroedmeester voor het platte land' (Obstetrician for the countryside) in May 1858 and August 1859, at Haarlem. For about one year he was physician in Jisp, North Holland. At the end of 1860 Van Rijgersma accepted a position on the island of Marken in the former Zuiderzee (now IJssel Lake). Here he married with Maria Henriette Gräfing on 14 April 1861, she was born in Amsterdam. A son Hendrik Eling (1862) and a daughter Marie Catharina (1863) soon joined their parents.

The Netherlands abolished slavery in the colonies of the East and West Indies on the first of July 1863. For that reason the Dutch government wanted physicians on the islands of the Netherlands Antilles, so Van Rijgersma applied for one of these places. He was appointed at Dutch St. Martin (the northern part belongs to France). The contract stated that his salary was 2000 guilders per year, and after twenty years he would receive a state pension. In addition he had the right to treat private patients.

The Van Rijgersma family (the doctor, his wife and two children) left Holland in September 1863 with the 'Columbus', the voyage went via the main island of Curaçao to St. Martin. His love for natural sciences was a special reason why Van Rijgersma wanted to go to the tropics. Being a physician he had enough knowledge of zoological disciplines like anatomy and physiology. Also botany was of great importance because of the medicinal plants, and since his father was a pharmacist, much of that science was learned at home.

At St. Martin doctor Van Rijgersma practised in the Back street (fig. 2) of the capital Philipsburg. Soon after his arrival he started to collect shells, which was his main hobby, and other animals. A few years later he wrote to professor Pieter Harting of the University of Utrecht for information to obtain a microscope. He received the instrument in 1866, and mailed a crate with bird-skins and fishes from St. Martin to the Zoological Museum in Utrecht.

In the meantime the family kept growing as in 1865 another girl, Anna Eliza Martina Philipina, was born, and the third daughter Ada Helena Hortensia arrived in 1867. Also in the last mentioned year a French priest, father J. Kohlmann, was appointed chaplain at Marigot, the capital of French St. Martin. Kohlmann was an amateur entomologist, so he shared an interest in zoology with Van Rijgersma; they became friends and exchanged parts of their collections: insects for molluscs.

In the 19th century the economy of St. Martin was based upon the cultivation of sugar cane and the exploitation of salt pans. During 1868 the director of the Salt company, mr. T. van Stolk from The Hague, visited St. Martin and met Van Rijgersma. Stolk admired the doctor's collection of natural history specimens, and he advised him to get in touch with the entomologist S. C. Snellen van Vollenhoven of the 'Rijksmuseum van Natuurlijke Historie' in Leiden. Correspondence started and lasted several years, resulting in an exchange of several parcels of Antillean insects for a collection of shells from the museum in Leiden (Gijzen, 1938:327).

Also in 1868 Van Rijgersma came in contact with the Academy of Natural Sciences in Philadelphia, this institute elected him as a Correspondent (cf. Coomans & Coomans-Eustatia, 1988: fig. 4). The relation with the Academy has been of great importance to zoology and paleontology of St. Martin and nearby islands. For a number of years Van Rijgersma collected animals and fossils, which were shipped to Philadelphia. The specimens were studied by American scientists and the results were published in a variety of articles. Many new species for science were described from the material, and in this way Van Rijgersma had contributed greatly to the zoological knowledge about St. Martin (Holthuis, 1959). The connection between the Academy of Philadelphia and Van Rijgersma was established via the famous zoologist Edward D. Cope, who named two animals after him; the fish *Ocyurus rijgersmaei* and the snake *Alsophis rijgersmaei*.

During 1868 Van Rijgersma painted sixty watercolours of flowering plants from St. Martin. The sketchbook with these beautiful watercolours and the descriptions of the plants was discovered in the United States by the present author in 1964. It proved to be the first illustrated document about the flora of the Netherlands Antilles. The complete manuscript was published in full colour, entitled 'Flowers from St. Martin, the 19th century watercolours of westindian plants painted by Hendrik van Rijgersma' (Zutphen, De Walburg Pers, 1988). This book includes chapters on Van Rijgersma's life and work, the history of Antillean botany, and the vegetation of St. Martin.

In March 1869 Van Rijgersma's younger brother Sigefridus emigrated from Holland to Argentina to become a farmer, he passed by at St. Martin. The following year correspondence and exchange of shells started with collectors in the USA and the Virgin Islands. Amongst them was Robert Swift of St. Thomas. Van Rijgersma visited him after the hurricane season of 1870.

Van Rijgersma was elected Corresponding Member of the Conchological Section of the Academy in Philadelphia in 1871. The letter with the announcement (fig. 5) was found in his correspondence, whereas his answer is still kept in the Archives of the Academy (Coomans, 1974: fig. 6). The contact with shell collectors was increased with new friends in Canada and at Guadeloupe.

Although Van Rijgersma had a busy life with children and biological work, the doctor did not neglect his medical duties. Sometimes he also took care of patients on the nearby island St. Barths, which was a Swedish colony at the time. When in 1871 doctor Heinrici had become mentally ill, Governor Ulricht of St. Barths asked Van Rijgersma to take care of his colleague. Van Rijgersma always gave his medical advises at St. Barths free of charge, therefore he was awarded a gold medal by King Karel XV of Sweden. It was received in 1872. More on Van Rijgersma's medical work is discussed by Coomans (1973) and Glasscock (1985: 113-115).

The fifth baby was another girl, Trijntje de Tempe, born in 1871; whereas in January 1873 child number six arrived, the second son, who was named after his uncle Sigefridus Gardengius. By that time Van Rijgersma was living at St. Martin for almost ten years. He had become a well to do man and could afford to make trips to several islands (fig. 6). He was respected as the physician of the island and had a good social life. His research in natural sciences offered much pleasure and made him known in biological circles of the area. With his artistic talents Van Rijgersma was able to make watercolours, a difficult technique of painting, of plants and shells from the Antilles.

Except for his eldest son Hendrik, who died at the age of 45 years because of lead poisoning, all other children were healthy and reached ages from 69 to 89 years. But doctor Van Rijgersma himself became serious ill in 1873 and therefore he was permitted a one-year sick leave to the Netherlands. The family left for Holland in April. During his furlough the Van Rijgersma couple celebrated their 12½ years wedding anniversary in October 1873. In the same month he had his photograph taken in Amsterdam (see frontispice). Prints of this picture were sent afterwards to his biological friends in the USA and the Antilles.

From some remarks in a notebook, found in his belongings, we conclude that Van Rijgersma had paid a visit to the Zoological Society in Amsterdam. This society kept the 'Artis' Zoo, an Ethnographical and a Zoological Museum. In the Artis Library he had made annotations on the literature of westindian marine animals. When in Europe, Van Rijgersma also became a member of the Belgian Malacological Society.

Van Rijgersma had a physical checkup in January 1874 and he was considered in good condition, therefore the family returned to St. Martin in March with the brig 'Santa Rosa'. Only the eldest son Hendrik, being partly deaf, remained in Holland with relatives, to learn the job of house painter. Back in St. Martin the seventh and last child was born, named Cornelis Washington.

Van Rijgersma renewed his correspondence with fellow shell collectors, to which new contacts were added in America, England and Brussels. Jules Colbeau, secretary of the 'Société Malacologique de Belgique', had asked him to publish in the Annales of the Society. Perhaps for this reason Van Rijgersma started in 1875 with a manuscript on the marine molluscs of the West Indies. He wrote it in a sketchbook, illustrated by himself with beautiful watercolours of shells from his collection. Many species were found on St. Martin, some are from other islands, which he had acquired by exchange. The shell manuscript is comparable to his work on plants in 1868, however, there was no systematical order in the botanical manuscript. In the shell work he discussed over 80 species; it was not finished but sixteen families have more or less completely been treated.

On 15 February 1876 Van Rijgersma bought the estate 'Little Bay'. It must have been a former suger cane plantation, as the Dutch part of St. Martin had almost one hundred plantations in the 17th to 19th centuries. A picture of the estate was published before (Coomans c.s., 1988: fig. 5). I was informed by Ineke Peeters-Willems of Aruba, a former resident of St. Martin, that she had found in 1976 the ruins of 'Little Bay', situated between Fort Hill and Little Bay Lagoon. At present this place in Little Bay Valley is used as building-site. Van Rijgersma paid 2000 guilders for the estate, this is equal to his salary for one year as governmental physician. In addition he had an income from the treatment of private patients. He was allowed this extra money to a maximum of one thousand guilders per year, but it is known that he received more. Anyhow, he was able to save about one thousand guilders each year.

No scientific activities or correspondence are known for 1876, the illness must have struck him again, resulting in his death on 4 March 1877. Doctor Van Rijgersma had reached the age of 42 years and 2 months. His death certificate (cf. Coomans, 1974: fig. 8) does not indicate the cause of death.

Several months later, in August 1877, an inventory was made of the belongings of Van Rijgersma and his wife. It mentioned four cases with shells and one with stuffed birds; medical instruments and supplies, also a book case containing 80 volumes of medical and other books. A microscope, which was used for his medical practice and biological research. Next to a barometer, extremely useful to predict the tropical hurricanes of the Lesser Antilles (July-October), he also had a telescope to study celestial events. He owned some cattle: two cows, a calf, a horse, a dunkey, goats and poultry. Therefore the family could supply its own milk, eggs and meat. The horse was used for the doctor's house calls. There were no valuable items on the list, in the tradition of the Dutch protestant religion the Van Rijgersma family lived simple and thrifty.

Van Rijgersma was buried at the Dutch Reformed Cemetery, now called the Cul-de-Sac Graveyard. His grave is still there in the shadow of a large tamarind tree, amongst other tombstones, some of them over two centuries old, containing the bodies of well known sons and daughters of St. Martin.

When the significance of doctor Van Rijgersma was rediscovered by Holthuis (1959, 1961), the government of St. Martin has honoured the former physician of the island on special occasions. On 20 November 1974, when the present author defended his thesis about the life and malacological work of Van Rijgersma, Lt. Governor R. O. van Delden put flowers on Van Rijgersma's grave (fig. 3).

Fourteen years later, on 3 September 1988, when the botanical manuscript was published as 'Flowers from St. Martin', Lt. Governor R. R. H. Richardson placed a bouquet on the grave, and so did the President of the Council of the Arts, Camille Baly, together with the authors.

Fig. 3. *Lt. Governor R. O. van Delden of St. Martin placed flowers on Van Rijgersma's grave, 20 November 1974, when the author defended his thesis at the University of Amsterdam. (Courtesy Beurs- en Nieuwsberichten.)*

After her husband's death, mrs. Van Rijgersma remained on
St. Martin with her children. In 1893 the family emigrated to the
United States and lived in Brooklyn, N.Y. (Daughter Ada returned to
St. Martin and got married to Josiah C. Waymouth in 1899). Mrs. Van
Rijgersma took along the shell collection of her late husband, his
illustrated manuscripts of plants and molluscs, the gold medal from
Sweden and many papers (official documents, letters, photographs,
etc.). She passed away in Brooklyn in 1906, almost thirty years after
doctor Van Rijgersma.

The present author was living in Brooklyn from 1960 untill 1964. In
the spring of 1964 I came in contact with descendants of doctor Van
Rijgersma, after searching telephone directories. At that time all his
children had died, but I met two granddaughters and the widow of
Van Rijgersma's son Sigefridus. The granddaughters, Ada
S. M. Johnson-Waymouth and Henrietta E. Reed-Waymouth, were
born at St. Martin, from the marriage of Ada H. H. Rijgersma to
J. C. Waymouth. These ladies supplied information about their
grandfather, they were also in the possession of a photograph of
doctor Van Rijgersma, and his gold medal. Helen van Rijgersma-Lang
was the second wife of Sigefridus, she kept in her house at Norwalk,
Connecticut, a box with the documents of doctor Van Rijgersma. All
these papers were donated to the present author and used for his thesis
(1974). Afterwards they were placed in the manuscript collection of
the library of the University of Amsterdam.

For many years Van Rijgersma's illustrated sketch books on plants
(1868) and shells (1875) were hold by his son Sigefridus. Finally he
presented them to his physician W. H. N. Johnson M.D. in Norwalk.
When I visited doctor Johnson he showed me the sketchbooks with
beautiful watercolours, together with some letters.

Van Rijgersma's manuscript was the first illustrated document on
the molluscs of the Netherlands Antilles. Its place in the history of
malacology will be discussed in the following chapter.

List of Shells collected by the late Dr. van Rijgersma of the Island of St. Martin, West-Indies and Catalogued according to their Genera Showing the quantity of each & where found.

Class I Cephalopoda
Order I Dibranchiata
  Section A. Octopoda.
    Family I Argonautidae.
      1 Argonauta Argo Lin: East-Indies.
  Section B. Decapoda.
    Family III Teuthidae.
      1 Sepioteuthis. St Martin W.I.
    Family VI Spirulidae.
      Spirula Peronii Lt. St Martin W.I.
      (large lot)
Order II Tetrabranchiata.
  Family I Nautilidae.
    2 Nautilus radiatus
Class II Gasteropoda.
Order I Prosobranchiata.
  Section A. Siphonostomata.
    Family I Strombidae.
      1 Strombus. Lin. South America.
      1 " Galateus (large) Pacific Coast.
      1 " Latissimus Lin.
      1 " Latirostris. Word.

Fig. 4. *First page of the 'List of Shells collected by the late Dr. van Rijgersma of the Island of St. Martin', which was sent to the Rijksmuseum van Natuurlijke Historie in Leiden in 1885. (Courtesy Dr. W. Backhuys.)*

HISTORY OF MALACOLOGICAL RESEARCH ON THE NETHERLANDS ANTILLES

Early history. The Carib and Arowak Indians which inhabited the Antilles in precolumbian times had already discovered the landsnails and the shellfish of the Caribbean Sea as useful natural products. The island 'Margarita' was named by Columbus after the pearls that were gathered from the Westindian pearl oysters by the Indian population.

The first European travellers to the Antilles were amazed by the colourful shells which are found on the tropical beaches. They took the nicest specimens home to be placed in the curiosity cabinets of the 16th and 17th centuries in Europe. The decorative shells were used by artists in their flower composition on still lifes.

The Reverend Teenstra (1836-1837: 261-262, 313) was excited by the many beautiful shells which he collected during a walk along Great Bay on St. Martin; at home he placed them into a specially made box with compartments. Twenty years earlier the schoolteacher Van Paddenburg (1819: 44-45, 61-62) described the edible oysters from the island of Curaçao. In another work about Curaçao, from the hand of the reverend Simons (1868: 150-151), a list of plants and animals was supplied as an addendum. The list was composed by the governmental physician N. Anslijn, who mentioned 28 species of molluscs. Both the Latin and vernacular names (Dutch and some in Papiamentu) were given; they were discussed by Coomans (1964).

The Danish shell collector Krebs (see page 32) published in 1864 a booklet on the Westindian marine shells. He included 118 species of gastropods and 3 bivalves from St. Martin; these shells were also discussed by the present author (Coomans, 1963).

When Van Rijgersma arrived at St. Martin in 1863 he started to collect shells, and during fourteen years he assembled an enormous collection with thousands of specimens and about 500 different species from this island. His (not finished) illustrated manuscript on the shells of the West Indies was written in 1875, and published in the present book. Van Rijgersma was the first malacologist who was interested in all molluscan groups of the Netherlands Antilles.

General works in which the complete mollusc fauna is treated, are the publications by Schepman (1915), Van Benthem Jutting on Curaçao (1925, 1927) and Coomans on St. Martin (1963 and 1967, 1974).

The activities of the Conchological Section of the 'Natuurwetenschappelijke Werkgroep Nederlandse Antillen' resulted in two booklets on the molluscs of Curaçao by De Jong & Kristensen (1965, 1968). The Department of Malacology of the Institute of Taxonomic Zoology (University of Amsterdam) issues a series 'Studies on West Indian Marine Molluscs' (nos. 1-11, 1984-1988), including articles on the Netherlands Antilles.

Land Snails (Pulmonata). Malacological research about the Netherlands Antilles started during the second half of the 19th century. Especially the landfauna of the Leeward Islands (Aruba, Curaçao and Bonaire) was of scientific importance because of the endemic species like *Cerion uva, Cistulops raveni, Gastrocopta curacoana, Microceramus bonairensis*, and several *Tudora's*. The results were published in short articles, in which one or a few species were described. The only exception is the publication by Mazé (1890), who discussed 48 non-marine gastropods from St. Martin, mainly collected by Van Rijgersma. The landshells of Curaçao and neighbouring islands werd described by Crosse & Bland (1873), Smith (1898) and Pilsbry (1903). All the literature on the landshells of the Netherlands Antilles from 1859 to 1906 was compiled by Vernhout (1914).

The American malacologist Burrington Baker stayed several months on the Leeward Islands and wrote extensively (1924) on the non-marine molluscs he had collected. He discovered several new endemic (sub)species, of which two, *Tudora muskusi* and *Cerion uva knipensis* were named after his host Mr. R. Muskus from plantation Knip on Curaçao. When the present author met Dr. Baker in 1960 he still spoke with enthusiasm about his stay on the Netherlands Antilles.

Other American malacologists who published on the landshells are Gould (1969, 1984) on the genus *Cerion*, and Clench (1970) about Saba.

In Holland mrs Van Benthem Jutting (1925) of the Zoological Museum in Amsterdam discussed the non-marine molluscs from Curaçao which were collected by her colleague Dr. C. J. van der Horst in 1920. From a zoogeographical point of view the landshells of the Leeward Islands were studied by Wagenaar Hummelinck (1940) in his thesis at the University of Utrecht. In later years Hummelinck kept studying this mollusc fauna (1963). He visited the islands a number of times and collected wherever possible. Parts of his material was studied by Haas (1960, 1962) and Venmans (1963). Some of Hummelinck's students published on the Cerionidae (De Vries, 1974) and Bulimulidae (Breure, 1974).

Hovestadt (1987) had collected on Curaçao and investigated the landmolluscs in relation to the historical zoogeography.

Within the group of the landshells or Pulmonates (with a lung and no gills) there is one family with an amphibious way of life near the seashore. This family, the Ellobiidae or Auriculidae, was discussed by Van Rijgersma in his manuscript (plates 61-64).

Marine gastropods (Prosobranchia and Opisthobranchia). The sea snails are by far the largest group of molluscs. Because of the great variety in shape and the colours of their shells, the prosobranchs are the most adored and wanted by shell collectors. Van Rijgersma has treated a number of families in his manuscript (plates 1-58).

The marine gastropods of the Netherlands Antilles, collected by Wagenaar Hummelinck, were surveyed by Coomans (1958). The collecting activities by a number of amateurs on Curaçao, Aruba and Bonaire during many years resulted in much valuable material, which was studied at the Institute of Taxonomic Zoology in Amsterdam, and published by De Jong & Coomans (1988). In total about 750 species were described of which 58 new to science.

Next to these larger studies, a score of articles about a single species or genus was written by a number of authors. To be mentioned here are the publications on *Latirus* by Melvill (1891), on *Echininus* by Kristensen (1965), on *Conus* by Van Pel (1969) and Vink (1974), on *Voluta* and *Cassis* by Van Pel (1971, 1974), on *Mareleptopoma* and *Euchelus* by Moolenbeek & Faber (1985, 1988), on *Cypraea, Teralatirus, Minipyrene* and *Pachybathron* by Coomans (1963, 1965, 1967, 1972, 1973, 1988) and on *Melongena* by Bruggeman-Nannenga & Wagenaar Hummelinck (1986).

The seaslugs (Opisthobranchia) generally have no shell. Van Rijgersma figured some of them in his manuscript (pls. 59-60). Two new species of opisthobranchs were collected by Dr. B. Sharp at St. Martin and described by Vanatta (1901). The Opisthobranchia from the Leeward Islands were the subject in the thesis of Engel (1925), and in some later studies (1927, 1936). More research about this group was performed by the Brazilian malacological couple Marcus & Marcus-du Bois Reymond (1963, 1970), they described a number of new species from the Netherlands Antilles.

Bivalves (Pelecypoda). The bivalved molluscs are living in freshwater and in the sea. Since freshwater is rather scarce on the Netherlands Antilles, only one species (*Eupera viridante*) is known from this environment on St. Martin. It was mentioned in the studies on non-marine molluscs (Mazé, 1890; Coomans, 1967:142).

The number of marine bivalves amounts to 150-200 species. There is no special literature about this group, but they are treated in the general works on the malacology of the Netherlands Antilles. Those from Curaçao were discussed by Van Benthem Jutting (1927) and by De Jong & Kristensen (1968); the bivalves from St. Martin by Coomans (1963, 1974).

Two families of bivalves, the Cardiidae or Heartshells, and the Verticordiidae were studied by Van Rijgersma (pls. 65-72).

Squids and *Octopus* (Cephalopoda). Van Rijgersma had donated two unidentified species of cephalopods from St. Martin to the Academy in Philadelphia, but at present these are no longer in their collection. Coomans (1974:208) mentioned 3 species from St. Martin.

Adam (1937) published on these animals from Bonaire and Curaçao. On one species new to Bonaire was reported by Moolenbeek, he mentioned a total of seven cephalopods from the Leeward Islands (1984).

Tusk Shells (Scaphopoda). This small zoological class is poorly represented on the Netherlands Antilles. Four species were discussed in Van Rijgersma's manuscript (pls. 73-74). In addition he might have been the collector of two new species, which were described by Pilsbry & Sharp in 1897 from St. Martin (cf. Coomans, 1974:207).

Chitons (Polyplacophora). Van Rijgersma knew nine species of chitons from St. Martin, they are called 'long back' on the island. A few chitons collected on Curaçao by Van der Horst were identified by Nierstrasz (1927). All those collected by Wagenaar Hummelinck in the Caribbean were studied by Kaas (1972); he mentioned 21 species from the Netherlands Antilles. On de radula and spines of some species from Curaçao was published by Righi (1968).

Fossils. The fossil shells collected by professor K. Martin in 1885 on the Leeward Islands were described by Lorié (1887). Many years later some Tertiary molluscs from Curaçao were studied by Van Regteren

Altena (1941); he also wrote on the fossil shells from the White Wall on St. Eustatius (1961). The Swiss paleontologist Jung (1974) described Eocene molluscs from Curaçao. In the same year the thesis of Buisonjé (1974) was published on the geology of the Leeward Islands, in which fossil bivalves and some gastropods were treated.

Applied Malacology. Professor Jan Boeke visited the Netherlands Antilles in 1905 to investigate the possibility for fisheries; he also discussed the oyster and mussel cultures (1907). By order of the Caribbean Marine Biological Institute on Curaçao the present author made a report about the economic aspects of the Antillean molluscs (Coomans, 1959).

Two Roman Catholic priests wrote on the Westindian pearl oyster and its pearls: Van Koolwijk (1884) on Aruba, and Euwens (1923) on those from Margarita, with a discussion about Aruba. Van Rijgersma mentioned the occurrence of pink pearls in the Queen Conch (*Strombus gigas*, plate 2).

In relation to medical malacology is the research on freshwater gastropods of the genus *Australorbis* (family Planorbidae) of vital importance. This snail is an intermediate host for the Bilharzia parasite. The distribution of *Australorbis* on the Netherlands Antilles was investigated by the physicians Emanuels (1933) and Van der Kuyp (1949, 1951).

The original population of the Caribbean Islands, the Amerindians, used molluscs for several purposes (Coomans, 1987). The animals were eaten, whereas the shells were manufactured into artifacts (household utensils, weapons, tools, ornaments, idols). Therefore, in the literature on archeology is often referred to molluscs and shells (Boerstra, 1982; Gould, 1971; Haviser 1987; Van Heekeren, 1960; Sypkens Smit & Versteeg, 1988).

Finally, on the vernacular names of the shells of the Netherlands Antilles (Papiamentu on the Leeward Islands, English on the Windward Islands) was published by Coomans (1970).

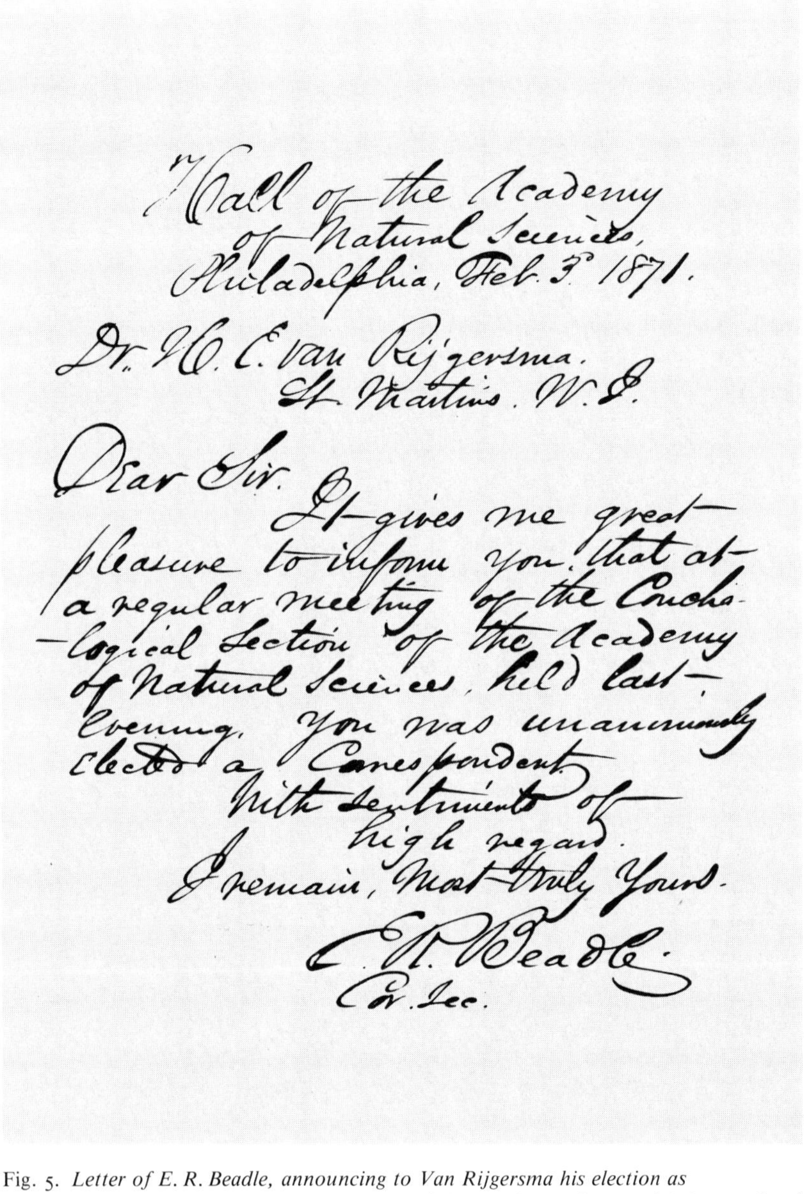

Hall of the Academy
of Natural Sciences,
Philadelphia, Feb. 3d 1871.

Dr. H. C. E. van Rijgersma.
St Martins. W. I.

Dear Sir.

It gives me great pleasure to inform you, that at a regular meeting of the Conchological Section of the Academy of Natural Sciences, held last evening, You was unanimously elected a Correspondent.

With sentiments of high regard.
I remain, Most truly Yours.

E. R. Beadle.
Cor. Sec.

Fig. 5. *Letter of E. R. Beadle, announcing to Van Rijgersma his election as Correspondent of the Conchological Section of the Academy of Natural Sciences, dated 3 February 1871.*

VAN RIJGERSMA AND MALACOLOGY

Shell Collection

Hendrik van Rijgersma's contact with shells dates from his childhood. From his correspondence it is known that as a boy he collected shells along the seashore, as his birthplace Lemmer was situated at the former 'Zuiderzee'. From sailors he bought tropical shells. Van Rijgersma must have loved the sea, because after one year of work in the country he practised for three years on the small island of Marken. But when the opportunity came to live on a tropical island, he applied for the position as government physician, so his love and talents for natural sciences could fully be developed.

After his arrival at St. Martin in October 1863 Van Rijgersma started to collect shells. Three years later he informed professor P. Harting of the University of Utrecht that he wanted to exchange shells with Dutch collectors; his collection of shells from St. Martin contained then 300 species. No evidence was found if he did exchange with collectors in the homeland, but he received Dutch shells from his brother in Holland. With father J. Kohlmann, an amateur entomologist and chaplain in French St. Martin, he exchanged half of his collection for insects from Guadeloupe. These insects were mailed later to the Rijksmuseum van Natuurlijke Historie in Leiden, for which he received 523 specimens of shells (111 species) in 1870. His collecting activities were not limited to St. Martin, he visited other islands (fig. 6) and picked up one hundred fossils on Anguilla.

Van Rijgersma became a Correspondent of the Academy in Philadelphia, to where he mailed animals of different zoological groups, for which he asked shells in return. After being elected a Correspondent of the Conchological Section of the Academy (1871), he also exchanged with private collectors in Philadelphia. It is not always known which species and how many specimens he received, but in some cases I found this information in his correspondence. R. Swift in St. Thomas sent marine molluscs of the genera *Cassis* and *Cymatium*, and more than 200 landshells from Venezuela and several Caribbean islands (Puerto Rico, Jamaica, St. Croix, St. Lucia, Bonaire). From French collectors on Guadeloupe his collection was enriched with material from France, Guadeloupe and Martinique. One of them, H. P. Mazé, published in 1890 on the non-marine molluscs of St. Martin, which he had received from Van Rijgersma.

Th. Bland in New York was interested in landshells, and Van Rijgersma supplied him with a collection from St. Martin. In return he mailed about 130 species, mostly from Cuba. Marine shells from the Bahamas and Barbados were received from governor R. W. Rawson.

During his sick leave in the Netherlands (1873-1874) Van Rijgersma contacted the English shell dealers Sowerby and Damon; he bought specimens from their stocks, and exchanged shells with them. He also offered duplicates for sale. In the correspondence I found the copy of a letter, in which he declared to dispose of a part of his shell collection, consisting of several thousands of specimens and between 500-600 species, for which he asked £50. In addition he offered birdskins, corals, sponges and Gorgonia (black coral) at 25 cents each species. It is supposed that the sale was not established, due to his early death in 1877. However, this letter gives a clue about the number of species he had collected at St. Martin, because his duplicates must have been mainly from this island.

From the correspondence and the manuscript it was figured that Van Rijgersma's shell collection amounted between 1500 and 2000 species, of which one third from St. Martin; and the total number of specimens between five and then thousand, the greater part from St. Martin.

At the time of his death (March 1877) Van Rijgersma had four wooden cases with shells. Not long afterwards his widow wrote a letter to Th. Bland in New York and asked his help to sell the collection in the United States. However, Bland advised her to sell it in Europe. When the Dutch botanist W. F. R. Suringar stayed on the Netherlands Antilles in 1884-1885 for research, he visited mrs Van Rijgersma at St. Martin. He was informed that the collections of shells and birdskins of her late husband were for sale. Suringar passed this message to F. A. Jentink, director of the Rijksmuseum van Natuurlijke Historie in Leiden. The latter wrote that the museum was interested and he asked for a catalogue of the objects. A complete list was made (fig. 4) and mailed to Leiden. (This handwritten list was recently discovered and obtained by Dr. W. Backhuys, who has deposited it in the 'Crosse-Foundation' at Oegstgeest. It will be discussed in a forthcoming article.) The museum selected 615 species (1202 specimens) from Van Rijgersma's collection, written on a second list. The majority of 387 species being from St. Martin, the remaining ones from twenty five other Caribbean islands. However, the shells were not sold to the

Leiden Museum, as no material from St. Martin is mentioned in the catalogue of the Museum's mollusc collection published by Horst & Schepman (1894-1908). Perhaps the sale was not established because of the price, or because only a part of the collection was selected.

From these two lists we have learned some facts about Van Rijgersma's shell collection: (a) it was arranged systematically; (b) it contained all kinds of molluscs, marine and non-marine, recent and fossil; (c) Van Rijgersma was a careful curator, keeping all lots separated, and well labeled with locality data.

Thus the collection remained at St. Martin. I was told by mrs. Helen van Rijgersma, daughter-in-law of doctor Van Rijgersma, that the collection was shipped to New York in 1893, when the family emigrated to the United States. It was packed in a number of crates. In America the collection was sold to a physician with a German name. From that moment on Van Rijgersma's shell collection is lost. Although many inquiries were made by the present author when living in New York (1960-1964), not a single trace could be found in American museums or with private collectors.

A few specimens, collected by Van Rijgersma at St. Martin, are kept in several American museums (e.g. the Academy of Natural Sciences in Philadelphia, the American Museum of Natural History in New York, and the Museum of Comparative Zoology in Cambridge). These shells were received via Van Rijgersma's exchange partners, like Th. Bland and R. Swift.

It is very unfortunate that the collection of Van Rijgersma has been lost, since it should represent the first complete collection of molluscs from one of the islands of the Netherlands Antilles.

Library

As was stated in the inventory made up after his death, Van Rijgersma had a book case with eighty volumes, mostly medical works. From his correspondence and manuscript it was possible to find out which biological books he owned (Coomans, 1974: 146-147). He had some general works, like the 'Handbook of Zoology' by J. van der Hoeven (1856-1858), and 'Leçons élémentaires d'histoire naturelle' by Chenu (1847). Only a few parts of 'Klassen und Ordnungen des Tierreichs' by Bronn, and of 'Histoire naturelle des Animaux sans Vertèbres' by Lamarck (2nd edition, 1835-1845).

Malacological handbooks with handcoloured plates are Sowerby's

'Thesaurus Conchyliorum' and 'A manual of the Mollusca' by
Woodward (1851-1856). Also the German edition of the classic work
by Knorr (1757-1772) 'Vergnügen der Augen' was in his small library.

From the Caribbean literature he possessed some works which are
now extremely rare: C. B. Adams (1849-1852) 'Contributions to
Conchology'; H. Krebs (1864) 'The West-Indian marine shells with
some remarks', and A. Schramm (1867) 'Catalogue des Coquilles et
des Crustacés de la Guadeloupe'. These three works were not
illustrated, but A. d'Orbigny (1839-1842 'Mollusques de Cuba' has
one volume of plates and two with text.

Van Rijgersma used P. P. Carpenter's work (1857) on the 'Mollusca
from Mazatlan' to compare the shells of the Eastern Pacific with those
from the Caribbean, since there is a close relation between both faunas.

Being a correspondent of the Conchological Section of the Academy
in Philadelphia, and a member of the Belgian Malacological Society,
Van Rijgersma had a number of volumes of the journals published by
these institutes. E. D. Cope, the secretary of the Academy, mailed him
reprints of the publications about the Antilles, for which Van
Rijgersma had collected the animals and fossils.

In total his library contained about 20 volumes of malacological
literature. From Van Rijgersma's research in botany (cf. Coomans
c.s., 1988: 31-32) was disclosed that he owned a copy of the 'Flora of
the British West-Indian Islands' by Grisebach (1864). There is no
information available what has happened to Van Rijgersma's library,
whether or not is was taken to New York when the family emigrated
to the U.S.A. in 1893.

Contacts and correspondence

During his stay at St. Martin Van Rijgersma was in correspondence
with other malacologists, they belonged to various countries: the
United States, Canada, England, France, Belgium, Denmark and the
Netherlands. Van Rijgersma exchanged shells with them, they
discussed mutual problems and helped each other with identifications.

In most cases the correspondence is known one-sided, from the
letters received by Van Rijgersma. However, some letters written by
himself are present in the archives of the Academy of Natural Sciences
in Philadelphia, in the Rijksmuseum van Natuurlijke Historie in
Leiden, and in the University Museum of Utrecht. His contacts are
discussed here in geographical order.

St. Martin. Van Rijgersma had a biological friend on the island: the French priest Joseph Kohlmann (Strasbourg 1834-Guadeloupe 1887). He was chaplain at Marigot, and interested in insects, especially beetles. Before and after his stay at St. Martin (1867-1875), Kohlmann lived in Guadeloupe, he established the contacts between Van Rijgersma with malacologists on that island.

Guadeloupe. The shell collector Arthur Bavay (France 1840-Paris 1823) was an apothecary in the French Navy, and interested in shells and botany (cf. Coomans c.s., 1988:30). He exchanged shells with Van Rijgersma. When Bavay returned to France via New Caledonia in 1873 their correspondence and exchange continued. Bavay has published mainly on the molluscs of Indochina, and on the families Marginellidae and Pectinidae.

Alphonse Schramm (France, ?-1875) was a custom inspector in French Guyana and Guadeloupe. Although mainly interested in marine algae, he also published on the crustaceans and molluscs of Guadeloupe (1867). The correspondence with Van Rijgersma was of short duration, in the year when it started (1871) Schramm lost all his belongings in a fire. A year later he returned to France.

The French naval officer Hippolyte Pierre Mazé (Brest 1818-Guadeloupe 1892) was stationed in Cayenne, Martinique and Guadeloupe. Together with Schramm he published on the marine algae of Guadeloupe between 1865 and 1877. Mazé also studied the landshells of the French Antilles, on which he wrote several articles: Martinique (1874), Guadeloupe (1883) and St. Martin (1890). The species mentioned in the last publication were collected by Van Rijgersma, and discussed by Coomans (1967).

Another French naval officer, Edouard-Auguste Marie (Tahiti 1835-Paris 1888) collected in many places where he was stationed and published more than ten articles on the molluscs of New Caledonia. Marie invited Van Rijgersma to come to Guadeloupe and he mailed shells of New Caledonia, France, French Guyana, Martinique and Guadeloupe. Van Rijgersma returned plants and shells from St. Martin, in addition he identified marine molluscs for Marie. Their contact lasted from 1875-1877.

Bonaire. The physician Gerrit M. D. Fock van Coppenaal (Alkmaar 1833-Amsterdam 1885) was Van Rijgersma's colleague on Bonaire. He kept an herbarium of which specimens were sent to Van

Rijgersma in 1874. Fock van Coppenaal surveyed the island for phosphate, and started a Freemason lodge on Bonaire.

Barbados. Sir Rawson William Rawson (1812-1899) was governor of Barbados from 1868 to 1875. He collected shells and had contact with Van Rijgersma from about 1872 to 1875, during which years Van Rijgersma visited him in Barbados.

St. Thomas. Robert Swift (Philadelphia 1796-St. Thomas 1872) worked as a merchant for ten years in Venezuela, and since 1835 on St. Thomas. He wrote in 1863 'Researches of the Virgin Islands' including a list with marine shells. The contact with Van Rijgersma began in 1870 and continued untill Swift's death. They exchanged shells, and Van Rijgersma has visited him on St. Thomas.

United States. Van Rijgersma's contact with the Academy of Natural Sciences in Philadelphia originated with a request by the secretary Professor Edward Drinker Cope (Philadelphia, 1840-1897). He published over 600 articles about fossil and recent vertebrates, including those from St. Martin, Anguilla, St. Eustatius, St. Kitts and Redonda, collected by Van Rijgersma. Many of the species were new to science, and therefore St. Martin became the island which was best known for a number of zoological groups in the 19th century. The correspondence between Van Rijgersma and Cope is known from both sides, it covers the years 1868-1869.

Also the secretary of the Conchological Section of the Academy, the Reverend Elias Root Beadle (1813-1879), corresponded with Van Rijgersma, from 1869 to 1875. Beadle had a very large private collection with many rare shells. Van Rijgersma was elected a Corresponding Member of the Section (fig. 5) and he mailed shells from St. Martin to the Academy.

William Laurence Mactier (1818-1888), a businessman in Philadelphia, was treasurer of the Conchological Section. He studied non-marine shells. His correspondence with Van Rijgersma took place in 1870, they discussed the exchange of molluscs.

An important contact was Thomas Bland (England 1809-Brooklyn N.Y. 1885). He had lived in England, Barbados, Jamaica, Colombia, and since 1855 in New York. Bland was specialized in Antillean and North American landshells, on which he wrote a number of publications. The correspondence with Van Rijgersma lasted from

1872 to 1877, they exchanged land and freshwater molluscs. Bland identified and commented on the shells from St. Martin, therefore his letters are of great significance for our knowledge of the malaco-fauna of this island.

Canada. A merchant from Halifax, named R. G. Haliburton, visited St. Martin in 1870 and met Van Rijgersma. Haliburton was interested in natural history, not especially in molluscs. However, it was Haliburton who established the contact of Van Rijgersma with R. Swift in St. Thomas, and with John Robert Willis (Philadelphia 1825-Canada 1876). The latter was schoolteacher in Halifax, he collected shells and published on the molluscs of Nova Scotia. He wanted to exchange with Van Rijgersma (1871) and offered Canadian shells.

Netherlands. In 1865 Van Rijgersma wrote a letter to Professor Pieter Harting (Rotterdam 1812-Amersfoort 1885) for information about a microscope, he also stated that he wanted to exchange shells with malacologists in Holland. Although there were shell collectors in the Netherlands in the last century, it seems that Van Rijgersma had no contact with them. Van Rijgersma did receive the microscope, and mailed a crate with bird-skins and fishes from St. Martin to Harting in 1866. No further correspondence is known.

At the 'Rijksmuseum voor Natuurlijke Historie' in Leiden, Dr. Samuel Constant Snellen van Vollenhoven (Rotterdam 1816-The Hague 1880) was curator of entomology. Van Rijgersma wrote to him (1868) and offered insects from St. Martin in exchange for molluscs from Holland or the East Indies. During 1869-1870 several parcels with insects were mailed to Leiden, and over 500 shells were returned to Van Rijgersma. Specimens of moths and beetles are still present in the museum. Snellen van Vollenhoven stated in a letter to Van Rijgersma that probably a number of new species could be found among them. Dr. Holthuis recently checked some entomological literature and found two records. Snellen (1875: 74-76) described *Simaethis aurofasciana* and remarked 'Op het eiland St. Martin door Dr. Reigersma gevonden'. Wulp (1882: 90) described *Urophora diaphana* 'from the isle St. Martin, presented by Mr. Rijgersma'.

Belgium. Van Rijgersma had become a member of the 'Société Malacologique de Belgique' at Brussels on the first of February 1874, during his European furlough. The secretary Jules A. J. Colbeau (1823-1881) asked to send shells from St. Martin for the collection of the Society. He also invited Van Rijgersma to publish in their Annales. We suppose that for this reason Van Rijgersma started in 1875 with his manuscript on West Indian molluscs, as he wrote to Colbeau on 1 June 1875 that he would like to publish in the journal. In Van Rijgersma's library there were six volumes (1874-1879) of the Annales of the Society.

England. During his furlough Van Rijgersma also contacted two malacologists in England. George Brettingham Sowerby III (1843-1921) was a publisher and shell dealer. Van Rijgersma bought shells from him between 1873 and 1875, and he offered molluscs from St. Martin, but Sowerby did not seem to be interested. On the relation between Van Rijgersma and Sowerby was published by Coomans & Pieters (1985).

Robert Damon (1814-1889) was a dealer in natural history specimens, he exchanged shells with Van Rijgersma. We suppose that Van Rijgersma offered Damon his duplicate shells and other animals from St. Martin for sale, as was mentioned before in this chapter.

Denmark. Hendrik Johannes Krebs (Denmark, 1821-1907) was a pharmacist who lived from 1843 to 1870 on St. Thomas, Virgin Islands. While travelling in the West Indies he collected plants and shells, and had visited St. Martin before Van Rijgersma arrived on the island in 1863. Krebs wrote 'The West-Indian marine shells with some remarks' (1864), a copy of this very rare publication was present in Van Rijgersma's library since he refers to it in his manuscript. Krebs mentioned 118 species from St. Martin, they were discussed by the present author (Coomans, 1963). The correspondence between Van Rijgersma and Krebs started when the latter was living in Denmark. In one letter of 1874, published in Coomans (1974: fig. 12) Krebs requested species of the genus *Scalaria (= Epitonium)*, to be studied by Mörch.

Otto A. L. Mörch (Denmark, 1828-1878) was a Danish malacologist. No letters from him were found in Van Rijgersma's correspondence, but according to Van Rijgersma's manuscript, Mörch had identified specimens for him. Although Mörch probably never was in the West Indies, he has published on the marine molluscs of this area (1875-1877); Van Rijgersma is not mentioned in these publications.

Travels

For his malacological and other biological research Van Rijgersma did not only make fieldtrips on St. Martin, he also travelled to other Antillean islands. From his manuscripts on the plants and shells, his correspondence and the publications by American zoologists it could be traced which islands he had visited (fig. 6).

In the first place the islands which are in sight of St. Martin: Anguilla, St. Barths and Saba; and further St. Eustatius, St. Kitts and Redonda. As far as known he had no biological friends on these islands, so he went there to collect shells for himself, and other animals and fossils for the Academy of Natural Sciences in Philadelphia. He also went several times to St. Barths in his profession as physician, to take care of patients on this Swedish island.

Van Rijgersma paid a visit to his malacological colleague Robert Swift in St. Thomas, one of the Virgin Islands, and he might have been on St. John and Tortola. Because he stated in his manuscript that he had seen the collection of governor Rawson in Barbados, he must have been overthere, and on his way the ship certainly anchored at several islands. Van Rijgersma was invited by E. A. Marie to visit him, but there is no proof if he went to Guadeloupe.

The Van Rijgersma family crossed the Atlantic Ocean three times: in 1863 from Holland to the West Indies, and later a roundtrip from and to St. Martin in 1873-1874. During at least one of these transatlantic journeys Van Rijgersma was on the Dutch Leeward islands Curaçao, Aruba and Bonaire. But it is questionable if he had much time to do any collecting on these three islands.

References in Malacological Literature

Van Rijgersma's work on zoology has already been discussed by Holthuis (1959: 72-76) and Coomans c.s. (1988: 19-21). His part in those studies was collecting the animals and fossils, from which many species new to science were described, and some named after their discoverer.

Although Van Rijgersma was in contact with many shell collectors, he is hardly mentioned in the malacological literature. The few references are summarized in my thesis (Coomans, 1974: 133-135). A few landshells from St. Martin were discussed by Bland (1871), Bland & Binney (1871) and Binney (1884, with figures). The most extensive

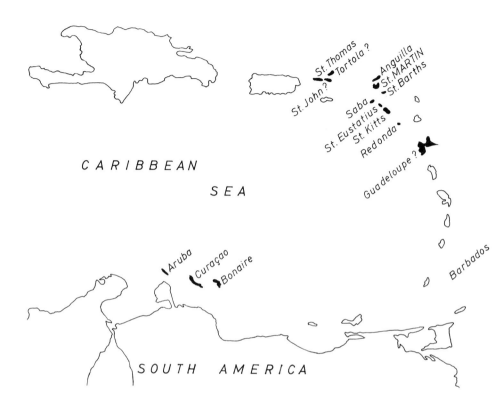

Fig. 6. *Map of the West Indies, indicating the islands visited by Van Rijgersma. (Drawing J. Zaagman.)*

was Mazé (1890), who was like Bland in correspondence with Van Rijgersma. Mazé mentioned 48 species from St. Martin, for the main part collected by Van Rijgersma and his friend father Kohlmann, this publication is not illustrated. In H. A. Pilsbry's 'Manual of Conchology' (second series vols. 11, 12 and 16, 1897-1903) a very few molluscs from St. Martin and Anguilla are treated.

The present author has published on Van Rijgersma's malacological work in several publications (Coomans, 1963, 1970, 1974). De Jong & Coomans (1988:38, pl. 2 fig. 171) have named a new gastropod species from Curaçao and St. Martin after Van Rijgersma: *Caecum rijgersmai*.

Manuscript on Westindian Molluscs

In 1875 Van Rijgersma started with a manuscript about the marine molluscs of the West Indies, based on his private collection and therefore mainly from St. Martin. When I discovered this manuscript in 1964 it was in the possession of W. H. N. Johnson M.D. in Norwalk, Connecticut. He had received it in 1963, together with a manuscript on the plants of St. Martin, as a gift from Van Rijgersma's son Sigefridus, who was his patient. Dr. Johnson kindly allowed me to photograph the manuscripts for further research and publication, but he did not want to part of the manuscripts. Dr. Johnson has passed away since, efforts to trace the present whereabouts of the manuscripts have failed, so they may have been lost.

The shell manuscript is bilingual, mainly in English and some parts in Dutch. It is illustrated by Van Rijgersma himself, 82 species of molluscs are drawn in natural colours, from specimens in his collection. A few watercolours and some pencil drawings were made after live molluscs with the animal in the shell; also some operculums and radulas were figured. In general each species is treated as follows: the scientific name – one or two colour drawings of the shell – synonyms of the name – description in Latin copied from the literature – distribution and occurrence on St. Martin – remarks.

The manuscript shows that Van Rijgersma was a good observer, he studied the shell, animal, radula and operculum, in addition he added ecological data. He compared his observations with the literature, was critical and remarked upon mistakes. He mentioned localitites with the distribution, and discovered that West Indian molluscs are related to those from the Eastern Pacific. In the family of the triton shells

(Cymatiidae) he found that many species from the East and West Indies are identical; whereas in the cowries (Cypraeidae) he described that difference in shell shape is due to sexual dimorphism. Without training in systematic zoology, Van Rijgersma's manuscript shows that he understood this discipline very well, also his nomenclature is correct.

Due to his illness Van Rijgersma did not continue the manuscript in 1876, thus it was not finished when he passed away in 1877. Only sixteen families have been treated.

The size of the pages in the manuscript is 21½ × 13½ cm. When possible Van Rijgersma made the shell paintings on natural scale, but the larger specimens were reduced, the smaller ones enlarged. The plates of the present work are printed in four colours, after colour slides which were made by the author in 1964, from the original watercolours by Van Rijgersma. The few pencildrawings, which are rather vague and therefore not suitable for reproduction, have been redrawn in ink by Jurrien Zaagman at the Zoological Museum in Amsterdam.

In the manuscript the text is written on the same page with the watercolours (cf. Coomans, 1974: pls. VI-XVII), but in the present book the text is removed from the plates and transcribed on the opposite page. Since Van Rijgersma had copied the Latin descriptions exactly from the books in his library, and thus not being his own text, they are not copied here again, but indicated between brackets. The abbreviations used in the manuscript refer to the literature he had available (see pages 27-28).

At the bottom of the textpages the present author has supplied additional information and comments, these are placed between brackets.

PLATES

Pectinibranchiata
Siphonostoma – Taenioglossa

Familie Strombidae
Genus Strombus

This family is very natural, the shell with an
expanded lip & deeply notched near the canal.
Operculum in our W. Indian species claw shaped
with a keelshaped line in the middle & not
serrated on the outer edge. Radula short,
median tooth 7 cusped, laterals slender
dentate hooks.

[upper figure] Radula of Strombus pugilis Lamk.
eene rij, the Median tooth more than 7
cusped, laterals some dentate, the first
simple. [After] Lovén.

[lower figure] Operculum of Strombus gigas

Strombus species opgegeven van de W. Indies.
   accipitrinus (Martini). costatus Gml. Antilles.
   alatus (Gml) S. pugilis Dilw. var.
   costo-muricatus Mart. raninus Gml. = lobatus Swainson –
      bituberculatus Lmk.
   dubius Sowb. een jonge schelp.
   gallus Linn. Oost & West Indie.
   gigas Linn. algemeen. Antilles.
   goliath Chemn.
   granulatus (Sowb.) Swainson. Westkust v. America, Panama.
   inermis Sowb. Hab. Bahamas.
   lentiginosus L. (Cuba D'Orb.) – Oost Indien.
   pugilis L. Barbad. Guad. St. Thomas, Tortola, St. Martin.

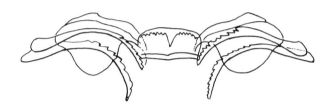

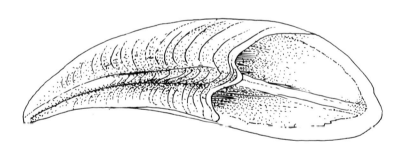

PLATE 2 [*Strombus gigas* Linné, 1758]

Strombus gigas Linn.
Lamk. An.s.verteb. vol IX No 1
Sowerby Thesaurus No 47

Algemeen verbreid over de WestIndien, varierende in kleur en vorm, de oude voorwerpen met mos en zeewier begroeid herbergen dan Caecum en Emarginula. Zeer jonge exemplaren zijn omstreeks een duim lang en gelijken veel op Triton.
Langwerpige ronde rooskleurige parels vind men, maar zeer zeldzaam in de schelp.
Het dier wordt door de armen gegeten, en dient ook voor aas. De schelp bij de visschers om er op te blazen nadat men er de top heeft afgeslagen. Volgens Gouverneur Rawson zijn de exemplaren van Barbados roodachtig en oranje, die van de Bahamas rooskleurig (delicate pink).

[English translation: Common in the West Indies, variable in colour and shape, the old specimens covered with moss and seaweed on which *Caecum* and *Emarginula* are living.
Very young specimens are about one inch long and very much resemble *Triton*. Elongate round pink coloured pearls are very rarely found in the shell.
The animal is eaten by the poor, and is also used for bait. The shell is used by fishermen to blow on it after the apex is cut off. According to Governor Rawson the specimens from Barbados are reddish and orange, those from the Bahamas are delicate pink.

Van Rijgersma seems to be one of the first malacologists, who mentioned the existence of pink pearls from the conch shell.]

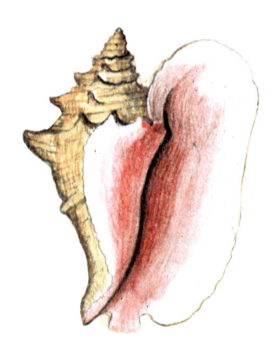

PLATE 3 [*Strombus gallus* Linné, 1758]

Strombus gallus Linn.
Lamk. An.s.Vert. vol. IX, spec. 5.
Sowb. Thesaur. Conch. No. 44.

[Latin description copied from Lamarck.]

Minder algemeen dan de voorgaande soorten en leeft ook op grootre diepte, St. Martin. Varieert, met eene van buiten steenroode schaal en van binnen roodachtig geel. Tusschen de jongen van Gallus en lobatus is niet veel verschil doch lobatus is altijd herkenbaar door de spilplooijen in de bovenhoek van de mond.

[Less common than the preceding species and also lives at greater depth, St. Martin. Variable, oiutside of the shell brick red and inside reddish yellow. There is not much difference between the juveniles of *gallus* and *lobatus*, however, *lobatus* can always be recognized by the spindle plaits in the upper part of the aperture.]

PLATE 4   [*Strombus costatus* Gmelin, 1791]

Strombus accipitrinus Martini
Strombus costatus Gml.
Strombus accipitrinus Lmk
Lmk Vol IX An.s.v. No 2
Sowerby Thesaurus Conch. Spec 45.
D'Orb Moll de Cuba, pag 119. Ala accipitrina Martini.

[Latin description copied from Lamarck.]

Veel minder algemeen dan de voorgaande schijnt
het toch over de geheele Antilles verbreid te zijn, en
varieert in groote en kleur, tusschen geel en
steenrood afwisselende, van binnen melkwit

Strombus dubius Linn.
vide Thesaur. Spc. 19, Vol 1, pag 29
schijnt het Jong van bovengenoemde soort te zijn,
doch in de Thesaurus zie ik niet de localiteit
opgegeven.

[Although far less common than the preceding species (= *Strombus gallus*) it seems to be distributed over the entire Antilles, and varies in size and colour, alternating between yellow and brickred, inside milky white.

Strombus dubius
seems to be the juvenile of this species, however, in the Thesaurus (= Thesaurus Conchyliorum, by G. B. Sowerby) the locality is not mentioned.]

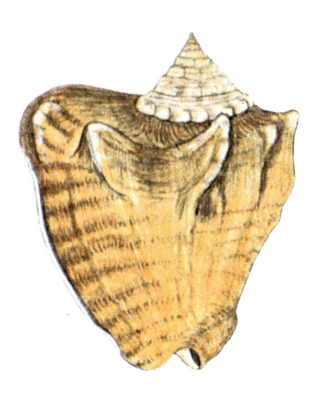

PLATE 5 [*Strombus costatus*, juvenile]

Strombus inermis Sw.
Sowb. Thesaurus Conch. pag 35, Spec 46, fig 113.
Strombe désarmé. Lmk.An.s.vert: pag 711. Spec. 34.

[Latin description copied from Sowerby.]

Wordt hier niet gevonden. 2 exemplaren van Gov. Rawson in mijn collectie, localiteit Bahamas. Sommige Conchyliogen beschouwen deze schelp als een varieteit van Str. accipitrinus.

[Is not found here. 2 specimens from Governor Rawson in my collection, locality Bahamas. Some conchologists considers this shell to be only a variety of *Strombus accipitrinus*.

At present *Strombus inermis* is considered a synonym of *S. costatus*, the shell is less heavy.]

PLATE 6 [*Strombus pugilis* Linné, 1758]

Strombus pugilis Linn.
Lamk An.s.Vertebr. Vol IX pag. 696, Spec. 12.
Sowerby Thesaurus Conch.: No. 33 pl. 8 fig 74.

[Latin description copied from Lamarck.]

Schijnt op grootere diepte te leven dan de vorige soorten, is hier zeer zeldzaam. Voorwerpen van St. Martin, St. Thomas, Tortola & Barbados in mijne verzameling. Heeft zeer veel overeenkomst met een schelp van Panama, de Strombus gracilior die echter lichter van kleur is en meer slender van vorm.

[Seems to live at greater depth than the preceding species, is very rare here. Specimens from St. Martin, St. Thomas, Tortola & Barbados in my collection. It much resembles a shell from Panama, *Strombus gracilior*, which however, is lighter in colour and more slender in shape.

Van Rijgersma was correct, the Caribbean *Strombus pugilis* and the Eastern Pacific *S. gracilior* Sowerby, 1825, are vicarious species.]

PLATE 7   [*Strombus raninus* Gmelin, 1791]

Strombus lobatus Swainson
Strombus bituberculatus Lmk An.s.v. Vol IX, Spec 6
D'Orb. Moll de Cuba, pag. 120.

[Latin description copied from Lamarck.]

Zeldzaam St. Martin, Barbados very common (gov. Rawson).
Het is volstrekt niet moeijelijk om gallus en lobatus van elkander te herkennen, de jonge schelp vereist echter eenige oplettendheid, de 2 knobbels zijn niet altijd even groot ontwikkeld, bij sommige zijn ze zeer kort, bij een ander exemplaar in mijne collectie van St. Thomas meer dan een centemetre lang.

[Rare at St. Martin, Barbados very common (Governor Rawson). It is not at all difficult to distinguish *gallus* from *lobatus*, however, the juvenile shell requires some attention, the 2 knobs are not always very well developed, sometimes they are very short, in another specimen from St. Thomas in my collection they are more than one centimetre long.]

Family Cypraeidae

The Cypraeiden are easily distinguished, by the form of their shells, no operculum and radula as Triton nl. 3-1-3.

Lingual dentition of C. helvola.
[figure after] Lovén.

Species of Cypraea mentioned from W. Indies:
bicallosa Gray. St. Vincent
cervus L. cervina Lmk. from Panama
cornea Gray = rosea Wood = costata Gml. Cape of Good Hope.
exanthemata Linn.
globosa Sowb = pilula Kiener
mus Linn.
nivea Gray.
pediculus Linn = sulcata Dillw.
quadripunctata Gr = rotunda Kiener
spurca L. flaveola Reve.
stercoraria L. Africa
succincta L. cinerea Mart. sordida Lmk.
suffusa Gray armandina Duclos
subrostrata Duclos Sandw. Islands
affinis Maratt.

[Van Rijgersma considered *Trivia* as a subgenus of *Cypraea*, therefore all species are united here in one list. At present the genus *Trivia* is placed in the family Eratoidae.]

[*Cypraea zebra* Linné, 1758]

Genus Cypraea Linn.
Shell more or less cylindrical.

C. exanthemata Linn.
[Latin description.]
Lmk An.s.vert. No. 2.
Sowb Thesaur. Conch. Spec 4
D'Orb. Moll. de Cuba No. 264.

Hab. West Indies, not rare, under Coral stones, his nearest analogue is C. Cervinetta from Panama but Dr. Carpenter sais that an examination of several hundred specimens (from Mazatlan) shows that the characters usually relied on tho separate the species are by no means constant. The yong ones have no ocellated spots but are only banded and more of a lead color.

C. zebra Linn.
C. plumbea Gml.
C. bifasciata Gml.   are all synonymes.
C. dubia Gml.

The radula of C. exanthemata is nearly as long as the shell (in Triton it is short) median and lateral theeth tricusped hooks.

[Van Rijgersma misspelled the name of *Cypraea exanthema*, it is now considered a junior synonym of *C. zebra*. Both names were described by Linnaeus.]

[*Cypraea cinerea* Gmelin, 1791]

Luponia Gray. Shell pyriform.

Cypr. cinerea Gml.
C. succincta Linn. M.L.U. 575. No 197.
C. cinerea Gml. Lmk Spec 22. C. sordida Lmk No 24.
C. translucens Gml. Syst. Nat. p. 3403. 1790
D'Orb Moll de Cuba No 267. C. cinerea. Gmelin.

[Latin description copied from Lamarck.]

Common. St. Martin and other Islands.
Specimens from Barbados oblong cylindrical,
they differ very much according their age,
cinerea are the young & sordida the old
specimens agreeing with Lamarck description,
Some are oblong other ovate: and may be
the difference in the Sexes.

[Van Rijgersma had guessed very well that the size of the shells in Cypraeidae is related to the sex of the animal.]

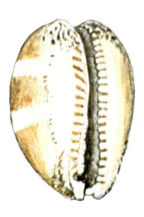

PLATE 11 [*Cypraea spurca acicularis* Gmelin, 1791]

Dorsal margins pitted.

Cypraea spurca Linn. var flaveola.
C. acicularis Gml.
C. flaveola Lam. spec 42.
C. spurca Sowb Thes. 131.
D'Orb. Moll de Cuba No 266.
[Latin description copied from Sowerby.]

loc. St. Martin not common but found at mostly all the West Indian Islands. Cape verd. Mediterranean, Indian & Pacific Ocean-Sowb. Méditerranée aux Iles Canaries et aux Antilles – D'Orb.
Our shell is the var. flaveola and only differs a little in the colors, having the under part pure white and not yellow as those from the Canarian Islands. The shell here depicted is one of the largest out my collection.

C. bicallosa Gray.
[There was no figure of this species. The Latin description was copied from Sowerby.]
Loc. St. Vincent. West Indies.
Of this very rare shell I have seen only one in the collection of Gov. Rawson W. Rawson, Barbados.
C. aubreyana Jousseaume appears to be the young. Vide Thesaur Conch fig. 529, 530.

[Van Rijgersma gave a correct description of the two subspecies of *Cypraea spurca*, but he was wrong about the identification. The Caribbean subspecies with the white ventral side is *Cypraea spurca acicularis*, the Mediterranean subspecies has a yellow ventral side and should be called *C. spurca spurca* (syn. *spurca flaveola*).
On *Cypraea surinamensis* Perry, 1811 (synonym *C. bicallosa*) was recently published by Coomans, 1988.]

PLATE 12 [*Cypraea mus* Linné, 1758]

Aricia Gray
Shell greatly thickened at the sides,
base flattened, back gibbous.

Cypraea mus Linné.
C. mus Lamk An.s.vert No 12
Sowb. Thesaur spec 48
D'Orb Moll de Cuba no 265.

[Latin description copied from Lamarck.]

loc. Curaçao, rare.

[On the distribution of this species was published by Coomans in 1963, from which was concluded that the locality Curaçao is not correct. *Cypraea mus* is living at the coast of Colombia and western Venezuela.]

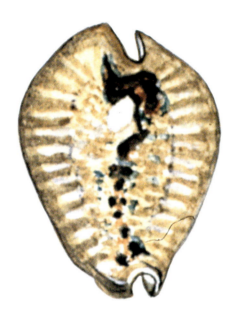

[Family Eratoidae]

Subgenus Trivia
Shell small, funt lirate, back with ribs or tubercles.

Cypraea quadripunctata Gray [1827]
C. quadripunctata Gray. Zool.Jour. p. 368.
C. rotunda Kiener Coq.viv. p. 141
Lamk.An.s.vert. page 569 spec 101. C. 4 punctata
D'Orb Moll de Cuba No 270.

[Latin description copied from Lamarck.]

Loc. West Indian Islands. St. Martin common. Philippines.

Cypraea suffusa Gray.
Trivia suffusa Gray Desc Cat.Cyp pag 16. 1832.
C. armandina Duclos.
C. suffusa Thesaur Conch plate XXXIV. fig 444, 445.
Lamk. An.s.vertebr: page 566, spec 97.

[Latin description.]

loc. West Indies. St. Martin, common.

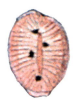 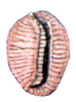

Cypraea sulcata Dillw.
C. sulcata Dillw. (non Gask.) Cat. 1, p 466. 1817.
C. pediculus Lin. Lamarck page 541, No 64.
C. pediculus Linn. D'Orb Moll de Cuba. Spec 269.

[Latin description copied from Lamarck.]

loc. found plentifully in the West Indies, St. Martin, Guadeloupe, St. Thomas, Barbados etc. Rumphius in his Amboinische Rariteits Kamer blaz. 118.. 1705 was the first who applied this name for the East Indian shell. Linnaeus used the same name for all the smal Triviae from East & West Indies and Europe. The East Indien species is therefore the pediculus, not oryzae Lmk. and the Lamarck name pediculus for our shell should be sulcata Dillw. by priority, although the name pediculus is now in generall use, it varies very much in sides and in colors.

labiosa Gask.
coccinella Lmk.
cimex Liegh Owen are all varieties.
Vide Thesaurus Conch. fig 429-438.

Cypraea nivea Gray
D'Orb Mollusq de Cuba. page 94. No 271.
Sowb. Thesaur. Conch. fol. 46, Spec 161, fig 468, 469.

[Latin description copied from Sowerby.]

loc. St. Martin, W. Indies, also subfossil from Barbados,
not common.
Manilla Sowb. Thesaurus.

[The species of the upper figure is now identified as *Trivia pediculus* Linnaeus, 1758.
The white *Cypraea nivea* of the lower figure is presently known as *Trivia nix* Schilder, 1922.]

[Trivia leucosphaera & antillarum]

Cypraea globosa Gray
C. globosa Gray. Desc. Cat. pag 14, 1832.
C. pilula Kiener, Coq. Viv. pag. 151, pl. 54 fig 2.

Cypraea subrostrata Gray
C. subrostrata Gray, Zool Journ III p. 363. 1827.
Sowerb. Thesaurus Conch. fol 48. Spec. 169.

[Latin description copied from Sowerby.]

Exept color there appears to be very little difference between this and globosa, they are of equal size and hight, but subrostrata has more ribs and the interstices are finely striated. – It may be that our shell is not the subrostrata, as Dr. Carpenter in his Catalogue of Mazatlan Shells fol. 379 sais: The West Indian shell (Bristol Mus) is of a richer colour, with the beaks less rostrate, and the dorsal sinus deeper and broader. Long. 25. lat. 18. alt. 16.
loc. St. Martin and other West Indian Islands, not common.
Mazatlan, Carpenter Catalogue spec 444.
Gallapagos Islands, Sowerby.

[Of the very small *Trivia* species on this plate the upper one is identified as *T. leucosphaera* Schilder, 1931. Van Rijgersma did not mention the locality.
With the species on the lower figure he agreed with Carpenter that the Eastern Pacific *Trivia subrostrata* is probably not identical with the Caribbean species. They were separated by Schilder, and the West Indian species is now named *Trivia antillarum* Schilder, 1922.]

[*Cassis madagascariensis* Lamarck, 1822]

[Family Cassidae]
Fam. Dolidae Brown. Cassidae.

Shell ventricose, spire short. Canal sharply recurved.
Operculum none or rudimentary, horny.
Radula short 3-1-3 not differing much from Strombus.
Species of the familie Cassidae supposed to be West Indian:
  Cassis abbreviata = from Panama.
  Cassis bisulcata Wagn.
  Cassis cicatricosa Desh. = inflata Shaw var.
  Cassis cornuta Linn, an East Indian shell = (Guadeloupe Schr).
  Cassis flammea Linn.
  Cassis granulosa Lmk = inflata Shaw, fide Reeve.
  Cassis gibba Gml = abbreviata.
  Cassis globulus Bolten = abbreviata.
  Cassis lactea Kiener = abbreviata var.
  Cassis Madagascariensis Lmk
  Cassis testiculus Linné
  Cassis tuberosa Linné
  Cassis ventricosa Martin = granulosa Lmk = tessalatum Chem.
  Oniscia Dennisoni Reve.
  Oniscia oniscus Linn.
  Pachybathron Gaskoin
  Dolium galea Linn
  Dolium pennatum M.
  Dolium perdix Lmk from the Sandw. Islands
  Ficula Swainson

Genus Cassis. Operculum small elongated.
Cassis Madagascariensis Lmk.
Lmk An sans vert Tome X page 20
[Latin description copied from Lamarck.]
[Figure of] Operculum of C. Madagascariensis, in and outside.
St. Martin, Guadeloupe. not rare.

[Van Rijgersma placed the genus *Dolium* (= *Tonna*) also in the family Cassidae. It is now in a separate family Tonnidae.]

Cassis tuberosa Linné.
Lamk An.s.verte. 1822. t.VII pag. 220. No 3
Buccinum tuberosum Linn. Gml. p 3473.
D'Orb Moll de Cuba p. 180. Spec 384.

[Latin description copied from Lamarck.]

[Figure of a] Young specimen

this shell differs from flammea in sculpture,
between old specimens the difference is very
apparent & constant. Sometimes used to cut out cameos.
Sold plentifully at the rate of 25 cents a pair as
ornaments and is called the Queen Conch.
lives on sandy flats nearly covered with the sand.
St. Martin June 1875.

[This is one of the few species for which Van Rijgersma used the vernacular name.]

PLATE 18 [*Cassis flammea* (Linné, 1758)]

Cassis flammea Linn
Lamk An sans vert 1822. t.VII pag 220. No 4
Buccinum flammeum Linn. Gml. p 3473. No 4
D'Orb. Mollusq. de Cuba page 180. 385.
Knorr. Verg. 3 t.10 fig 1, 2 an old specimen
Knorr. Verg. 4 t.4 fig 1 a young specimen.

[Latin description copied from Lamarck.]

[Figure of a] Young specimen.

Cassis flammea & C. tuberosa are quite distinct
the former is oval and is only 5 or 6 inches in
length while the latter is triangular and attains
a lenth of 10-11 inch. There is a uniform variation
in the sculpture which in C. flammea rather assumes
the nature of plicated wrinkles, the tubercles
are more numerous, smaller & more compressed.

[*Phalium granulatum* (Born, 1778)]

Cassis inflata Shaw. fide Reeve
C. ventricosa Martini. tessalatum Chemn.
C. granulosa Lmk. An s vert tom X pag 35. No. 20.

[Latin description copied from Lamarck.]

The Cassis granulosa group is very puzzling.
I have separated four types, of those found here.
One may be Cassis cicatricosa, because the
difference between inflata & cicatricosa is much greater, than between
inflata & his Panamanic analogue the C. abbreviata, of which
Prof. Adams says, it has the same remarkable
difference in form & sculpture.
Spec. from St. Martin 50 millm, one from St. Thomas.
80 mill. with very dark spots.
June 1875.

[Next to the shell Van Rijgersma also made a drawing of the fan shaped operculum.]

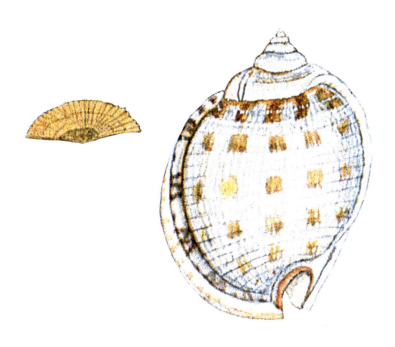

[*Phalium cicatricosum* (Meuschen, 1787)]

Cassis cicatricosa Desh.
Buccinum cicatricosum Gronov. Zoophyt. fasc 3.
Lamk. An sans verte. Tome X. pag 42. No. 29.
Cassis Granulosa Jun. Kiener
C. recurvirostris Gml.

[Latin description copied from Lamarck.]

This shell may be only a var. of C. inflata but some
think it quite distinct, it is more ovale, transparent,
and the surface is malleated.
from St. Martin, it is not the largerst out my collection
but as large as 70 mill.
I have nine; it is not at all a common shell.

PLATE 21 [*Cypraecassis testiculus* (Linné, 1758)]

Cassis testiculus Linné

Lamk An s.vertr. tome X, page 32, No 15.

[Latin description copied from Lamarck.]

A very common shell in the West Indies,
also on the Brasilian Coast & the coast of Africa,
according M. M. Webb & Berthelot (D'Orb. Moll de Cuba).
This [figure] is the largest shell from my collection, mostly smaller.
St. Martin Nord and East side of the Island on a coral or rocky bottom.
June 1875.

Pachybathron Gaskoin.
Shell small, oblong, striated with lines of growth; spire small, depressed, with channelled suture; aperture with callous denticulated lips, like Cypraea. – Woodward.
from the West Indies. Gov. Rawson who writes Barbados 27 April 1875:
'Among the Cassididae the only shell of rarity & interest that I possess is the Pachybathron of Gaskoin. I forget its specific name. It is very like a small Marginella & might well be mistaken for it. You may quote it on my authority'.

[Van Rijgersma discussed the genus *Pachybathron* with the Cassidae. It is now placed in the Marginellidae (cf. Coomans, 1972, 1973). Since he had no specimens available, there is no figure.]

PLATE 22   [*Morum oniscus* (Linné, 1767)]

[Family Harpidae]

Genus Oniscia Sowerby.
Shell with a short spire and a long narrow aperture, slightly truncated in front. Outer lip thickened, denticulated: inner lip granulated;

Strombus oniscus Linn. Syst. nat.
Oniscia oniscus Sowerby
Oniscia Lamarckii Desh; Lam: An s vert. Tom X pag 12.
Cassidaria oniscus Lmk. An.s vert Tom X, page 10

[Latin description copied from Lamarck.]

Hab. St. Martin, Cuba, Guadeloupe, St. Lucie, Barbados.
a very common West Indian shell the oniscia Lamarck in Desh & oniscus Sowerby appears to be the same shell,
my St. Martin specimens are all white, underneat.
Lenght about 23 millm.

Oniscia Dennisoni Reeve
[Latin description copied from Lamarck.]
Lamk An.s.v. tome X, pag 14.
Hab. Guadeloupe.

[Since Van Rijgersma did not figure *Morum dennisoni* (Reeve), this rare deepwater species was not present in his collection.
The genus *Morum* is now placed in the Family Harpidae.]

PLATE 23 [*Tonna maculosa* (Dillwyn, 1817)]

[Family Tonnidae]

Genus Dolium Lam.
Shell ventricose, spirally furrowed, spire small,
aperture very large, outer lip crenated.
no operculum. Woodward.

Dolium pennatum Mart.
Dolium perdix Lamk.
D'Orb Mol. de Cub. No 388.

[Latin description copied from Lamarck.]

Dolium perdix Lmk is from the Sandwich Islands and is different from our shell, which Mörch says is D. pennatum Mart.
a specimen from St. Martin, nat. size, which is thicker and heavier than a spec from St. Thomas 3 times larger. – common, rocky bottom. N.O. side of this island.

[For a figure of the radula see plate 24.]

[*Dolium* is a junior synonym of *Tonna*. Two closely related species are known: *Tonna perdix* (Linnaeus, 1758) from the Indo-Pacific, and *Tonna maculosa* from the West Indies. Some authors consider the Caribbean species a subspecies: *T. perdix occidentalis* (Mörch, 1877).]

PLATE 24 [*Tonna galea antillarum* (Mörch, 1877)]

Dolium galea Linn.

Lamk An s vert. tome X pag 139.

[Latin description copied from Lamarck.]

This Mediterranean species is found but selden at St. Martin, and mostly small and dead spec.
it appears to be very widely distributed from Barbados Guadeloupe & St. Martin, St. Thomas.

[Figure of the] Lingual dentition of Dolium perdix (Woodward).

[This species is found at both sides of the Atlantic; *Tonna galea galea* (Linnaeus, 1758) lives in the tropical eastern Atlantic and in the Mediterranean Sea, the subspecies *T. galea antillarum* is from the West Indies.]

PLATE 25 [*Bursa granularis* (Röding, 1798)]

[Family Bursidae]

Genus Ranella Lmk.
Shell with two rows of continuous varices, one on each side.

Ranella Cubaniana D'Orb.
No 358. Moll. de Cuba pag 165 pl XXIII. Fig 24

[Latin description copied from d'Orbigny.]

Hab. Cuba & St. Lucie D'Orb.
Several semifossil from Barbados.

Ranella crassa (Reeve) Dillw.
D'Orb Moll. de Cuba No 357
Ranella granulata Lmk. An.s. vertebr.

[Latin description copied from Lamarck.]

Hab. Guadeloupe D'Orb.
I have not seen it.

[The genus *Bursa* (synonym *Ranella*) is placed in the family Bursidae. The two species discussed on this plate are *Bursa granularis* (syn. *B. cubania* d'Orb.) which is figured, and *B. spadicea* (syn. *B. crassa*). Both species were not known to Van Rijgersma from St. Martin.]

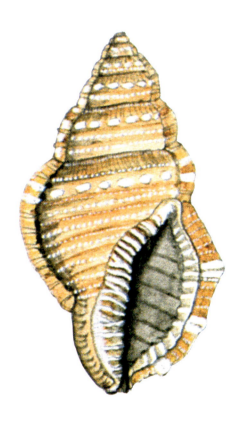

PLATE 26 [*Bursa thomae* (d'Orbigny, 1842)]

Ranella Thomae D'Orb 1848, Pl. XXIII, fig 23, 24.

[Latin description copied from d'Orbigny.]

Lmk An s.vert. Tome IX page 552
Ranella rhodostoma Swb.

I believe that the shells in general named R. rhodostoma are the same as this shell, rhodostoma is from Maksba l'une des Philippines, it is true D'Orb sais. Aperture alba: but may not this specimen be bleached and lost his colour? The specimens from the West Indies, named rhodostoma dont differ from the Thomae except the colour of the mouth being of a beautiful rose purpre in all his parts.
not common. St. Martin; Guadeloupe; St. Thomas & Barbados.

two other species of Ranella I find mentioned from West Indies
R. livida Reeve, Jamaica
R. ponderosa Reeve, Guadeloupe, Jamaica.
making the general number 6 Species:
R. crassa Dillw. R. granulata Lmk
R. cubaniana D'Orb.
R. livida Reeve
R. rhodostoma Sowb. R. Thomae D'Orb.
R. ponderosa Reeve
R. anceps Lmk.

[Van Rijgersma united the Indo-Pacific *Bursa rhodostoma* (Sowerby, 1835), with a reddish aperture, and the West Indian *Bursa thomae* (d'Orbigny), characterized by its purple aperture. Although they are related, we consider them as separate species.]

PLATE 27   [*Aspella anceps* (Lamarck, 1822)]

Ranella anceps Lmk.

[Latin description copied from Lamarck.]

I have received Ranella anceps from Mauritius it is much larger than our shell, and agrees with the picture given in Chenu Manuel de Conch.
Mr Swift of St. Thomas thinks our shell may be R. hastula Reeve.
loc. Anguilla, also St. Martins (with hermit crabs).

[This species is now placed in the genus *Aspella* of the family Muricidae.
Because of the white colour of the shell Van Rijgersma placed the specimens on a black cloth, pinned down on the table, before he made the drawing.]

PLATE 28 [*Cyphoma gibbosa* (Linné, 1758)]

Family Ovulidae

Genus Ovula Brug.

The shells of this genus Ovula placed by Dr. Bronn, Klassen und Ordnungen, with Cypraea in the family Cypraeidae, are a separate family named Ovulidae in the Catalogue of Mazatlan shells, following Dr. Carpenter not calling this family Amphiperasidae as American authors do. Dr. Theodore Gill has in the American Conchological journal pointed out the difference between the Cypraea's and Ovula's consisting principally in the habit of the animal living on the stems of Gorgonia's, the radula as not belonging to the taenioglossa & by the simple rolling of the shell itself.

Subgenus Cyphoma Bolten.
Ovula gibbosa Linn.

[Latin description copied from Sowerby.]

Ovulum gibbosum. Thesaurus Conch page 479, No 38.
A very common West Indian shell, from Curacoa –
Jamaica – Also Brasilian coast.
the loc. Panama in the Thesaur Conch is an error, the shells are mostly smaller and animal is very pretty with square yellow marks.

Augustus 1875

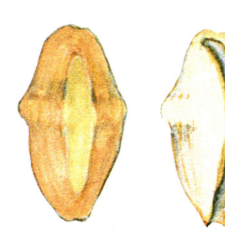

PLATE 29 *[Neosimnia acicularis* (Lamarck, 1810)]

Subgenus Volva Bolten 1798
Ovula aciculare Lmk An s. vertebr. Tome X pag. 472.

[Latin description copied from Sowerby.]

Thes. Conch II. pag. 477, pl 100 fig 43-46.
Hab. very common on the stems of Gorgonia flabellum.
Very different in colours violet, darker reddish purple, or very pale fawn or yellow.

O. Antillarum Sowb.
   C.Ic. pl. 14, spec. 64, 1865
   West Indies.
   I have not seen it.

O. subrostratum Sowb.
   Thes. pl.C. fig. 39, 40.
   Honduras bay.

O. uniplicatum Sowb.
   Thesaur. pl. 100, fig. 30, 31, 32.
   loc. South Carolina.

[Van Rijgersma had only specimens of the first mentioned species in his collection.]

PLATE 30   [*Cymatium femorale* (Linné, 1758)]

Familie Tritonidae [= Ranellidae]

Shell very much as by the Muricidae.
Operculum ovate, subconcentric, radula short, 3-1-3, much like Strombus & Cassis.

Genus Triton Lmk.
Shell with disconnected varices, canal prominent, lips denticulated. (Woodward).

Triton femorale Lmk.

[Latin description copied from Lamarck.]

Lmk. An s vertebr: Tome IX page 632.
D'Orb. Mollusq. de Cuba. N. 350.

a very common shell found at mostly all the islands.
Epidermis thin and smooth, at intervals beautifully erected and studdied with stiff hairs of a darker colour.
Length of my largest. millm 120.

[Next to the watercolour of an empty shell, Van Rijgersma also made drawings of a very young shell, and the live animal in its shell, with the hairy periostracum.
The family Tritonidae is now called Ranellidae (synonym Cymatiidae).]

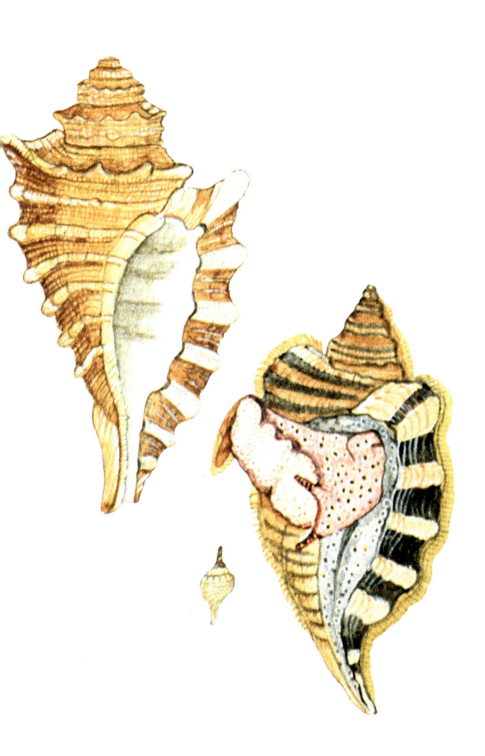

PLATE 31   [*Cymatium muricinum* (Röding, 1798)]

Triton tuberosum Lamk
Triton Antillarum D'Orb.

[Latin description copied from Lamarck.]

Lmk. An s v. Tome IX. page 635
D'Orb Moll de Cuba. No 352.
There appears to be no difference between the East Indian and our species except as D'Orb. has it 'mais elle s'en distingue par ses tours moins ventrus et moin anguleux'.
a difference only perceptable in picked species.
common. Cuba, Martinique, Guadeloupe, St. Thomas, Jamaica, St. Martin.

July 1875.

Triton Americanum D'Orb.

[Latin description copied from d'Orbigny.]

D'Orb M de Cuba pag 163 No 355.
I have seen one specimen in the Collection of the late Mr Robert Swift and one from Gov. Rawson of Barbados, the shell appears to be rare, and is perhaps nothing else than a straggler from South America, the Triton olearum L. as I find Tr. costatum Born mentioned from Guadeloupe in Mr Krebs list.

[The latter species, *Triton americanum*, which is presently known as *Cymatium parthenopeum* (von Salis, 1793) was not figured, as Van Rijgersma did not have a specimen in his collection. But from his remarks can be concluded that he visited his fellow collectors in St. Thomas and Barbados.]

PLATE 32 [*Cymatium pileare* (Linné, 1758)]

Triton pileare Linn.

[Latin description copied from d'Orbigny.]

Long 80 millm.

Triton Martinianum D'Orb. No 354 pag. 162.
Murex pileare Linn Syst nat ed 12
Our shell is called Martinianum by D'Orbigny on the account he
thinks that the Mediterr. spec. the olearium Linn. should be called so.
In the St. Martin spec. is the mouth not very red.
when fresh covered with the same form of Epidermis as femorale.
Some var. are called Triton aquatilis Rve.
Proc. Zool Soc. 1844

[Latin description copied from Reeve.]

[From this plate can be concluded that Van Rijgersma also studied the living animal.]

PLATE 33   [*Cymatium nicobaricum* (Röding, 1798)]

Triton chlorostomum Lmk
A. sans vert. Tom IX, pag. 636

[Latin description copied from Lamarck.]

Long 40 millm: M. de Cuba No 351.
My specimen is much larger than the one described by D'Orb, nearly 65 millm.
I have received one from Sowerby, Loc. Philippines.
St. Martin, Guadeloupe, St. Thomas, Cuba.

[Next to the shell Van Rijgersma has figured the operculum.
Cymatium nicobaricum is a senior synonym of *C. chlorostomum* (Lamarck, 1822).]

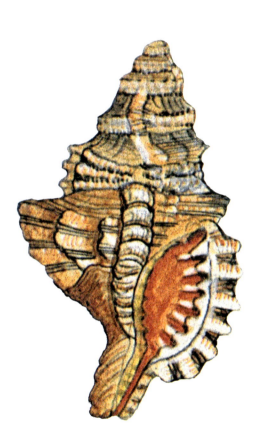

PLATE 34 [*Cymatium gracilis* (Reeve, 1844)]

Triton vespaceum Lmk.
Lmk An s.vert. page 636, No 19.
Triton quêpe de Mer. Triton vespaceum Lmk

[Latin description copied from Lamarck.]

Kiener. Spec des Coq. pag 18, no 13, pl 3, fig 2.

about half dozen specimen from St. Martin in my collection, name given me by Prof. Mörch.
most specimen with 5 whorls, this has 6.

July 1875.

[Although *Cymatium vespaceum* (Lamarck, 1822) is a West Indian species, the figure made by Van Rijgersma is evidently the closely related *C. gracilis*.]

PLATE 35   [*Cymatium caribbaeum* Clench & Turner, 1957]

Triton cynocephalum Lmk.

[Latin description copied from Lamarck.]

Lamk An.sans Vert: Tom. IX, page 631.
Length 60 millm. and smaller, common in St. Martin also from Guadeloupe, St. Thomas, Barbados etc.
Operculum large nearly closing the mouth.
Epidermis hairy & thin.

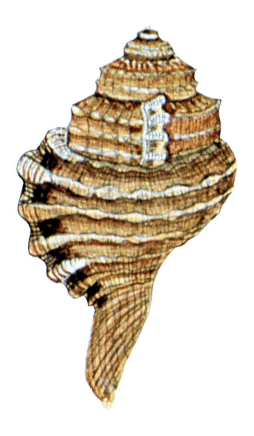

PLATE 36 [*Cymatium krebsii* (Mörch, 1877)]

Triton ficiformis Rve.
I have 7 specimens of this shell in my collection of which this is the largest and much rubbed, the small ones are younger and have these colours & Epidermis preserved: they look like the young of pileare, but the mouth is narrower and they are lighter of colours. I have not seen the diagnosis but the name is given me through the kindness of Govr. Rawson by Prof. Mörch.
Hab: St. Martin.

[According to Van Rijgersma's figure he obviously had *Cymatium krebsii*. This species was described by Mörch in 1877, Van Rijgersma compiled his manuscript in 1875, and therefore got another name from Mörch. Two mistakes were made by Van Rijgersma: *Triton fusiformis* was described by Kiener, not by Reeve; the name *Triton* 'ficiformis' Reeve is an error.]

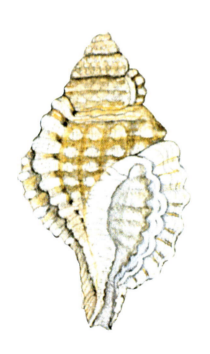

PLATE 37   [*Cymatium labiosum* (Wood, 1828)]

Triton labiosum Wood.
Index testac. supl pl 5, fig. 18
Triton rutile Mencke.
Loroisii Petit, Journ. de Conch. vol. 3,
pl 2, fig. 8. = T. rutilum Menke fide Rve.

[Latin description copied from the Journal de Conchyliologie.]

Long 21 m/m. Diam. 15 m/m. Journ. de Conch. vol 3 p. 53.
This species is not rare and varies much in size and colours. Some are of a reddish yellow, others dark brown; with or without varices; but mostly without.
Operculum ovate with apical nucleus.
Hab. St. Martin, Guadeloupe, St. Thomas, Barbados.

July 1875

Triton gibbosum Reeve.
Of this small and beautiful shell I have 3 spec in my collection and two very young ones appearently the young, not common, resembling a ranella
St. Martin

Augustus 1875

[*Cymatium gibbosum* (Broderip, 1833) is an Eastern Pacific species. Van Rijgersma's drawing looks as if it represents a juvenile specimen, of which we cannot conclude to which Caribbean species it belongs.]

PLATE 39   [*Charonia variegata* (Lamarck, 1816)]

Triton variegatum Lamk: var.
Murex tritonis Linn. Syst. nat.

[Latin description copied from Lamarck.]

Long 300 millm and more.
Our shell is not as elongated as the East Indian species, more coarse in make & sculpture.
(Triton marmoratus Lmk.)
See Knorr. Vergn. 5,t.5,f.l.
Not common. St. Martin, Guadel. St. Thomas.

Subgenus Persona

Triton cancellinum Desh.
Triton clathratum Lmk No 22 pag 637

[Latin description copied from Lamarck.]

Murex cancellinus Roissy Buf. Mol.
Murex mulus Dillw. Catal.

rare, one from St. Thomas, and a young from St. Martin in my collection.
from Tabego, Gov. Rawson.

[Van Rijgersma did not make a drawing of the lower mentioned species, which is presently known as *Distorsio clathratus* (Lamarck, 1816).]

PLATE 40

[This list summarizes all the species of 'Triton' known to Van Rijgersma from the 'West Indies'. It includes species which are placed now in different genera, like *Cymatium, Charonia* and *Distorsio* (fam. Ranellidae), and *Colubraria* (fam. Colubrariidae). Some of these are not living in the Caribbean, but belong to the Eastern Pacific fauna.]

Tritons mentioned from the West Indies
Americanum D'orb. = Olearium Linn ? W. In.
Antillarum D'orb = tuberosum Lmk W. Indies
Aquatilis Rve. = pilsare Linn ? W. Indies
Cariboeum D'orb. = Pisania
Chlorostomum Lmk W. Indies
Cantrainii Reclu = Murex pauperculus Adams
Costatum Born.= Olearium – W. Indies
Cynocephalum. Lmk W. Indies
eximius Rve.
femorale Lmk. W. Indies
gracilis Rve.
labiosum Wood: rutilum Menck Loroisii Petit W. Indies.
Lanceolatum. Kiener W. Indies
Mulus Dillw. Cancellinus Dest Clathratum Lmk W. Indies.
Martineanum D'orb = pileare
nobile Conr.
obscurum Reeve
parvum C.B. Adams.
pileare Linn W. Indies
pulchellum CB Adams. Jamaica
reticulatum Blain. from the Mediterr. Sea
rostratum M. = Cassidaria cingulata Lmk
testaceum Morch W. Indies.
tigrinum Brod. from Centr. America
variegatum Lmk. = W. Indies
vestitum. Hinds. from Panama.

PLATE 41 [*Colubraria obscura* (Reeve, 1844)]

[Family Colubrariidae]

Subgenus Epidromus.

Triton testaceum Mörch.
Of this not common shell I have a few specimen from St. Martin, and one from St. Thomas. I have not seen the diagnosis but the name given me by Mr Robert Swift. St. Thomas.

[Two species of *Colubraria* (synonym *Epidromus*) were placed by Van Rijgersma in the genus *Triton* of the family Tritonidae. They are presently separated into the family Colubrariidae.]

PLATE 42   [*Colubraria lanceolata* (Menke, 1828)]

Triton lanceolatum Kiener.
Triton lanceolatum. Lmk An s.verte. Tome IX p 647
Kiener Spec des Coq. p 27, No 21, pl 18, fig 1.

[Latin description copied from Lamarck.]

Not rare quite distinguisable from the Mediterranean spec.
the Tr. reticulatum Bl.
Habitat. St. Martin & St. John.
Porto Rico, Lmk. An s.v.
Guadeloupe Schramm.

PLATE 43 [*Conus regius* Gmelin, 1791]

Toxiglossa. **Family Conidae**

Genus Conus.
Shell inversely conical, aperture long and narrow, outer lip notched at or near the suture; operculum minute lamella.
groep. Coronated turbinated straight sided.

1. Conus nebulosus Solander.
D'Orb. Moll de Cuba. pag 115. Lam. An. sans
vert Tom XI p. 19; Thesaur. Conch Spec 44 fig. 61, 62.

[Latin description copied from Lamarck.]

One of the most common species found at all the West Indian islands, mostly smaller than the one here depicted from St. Martin.

Nov. 1875.

2. Conus cedo-nulli Brug.
Thesaurus Conch spec 43 Fig 64, 68.

[Latin description copied from Sowerby.]

found only one at St. Martin, into bad a state to be drawn.

[*Conus nebulosus* is a junior synonym of *Conus regius*.
It is doubted if Van Rijgersma had collected *C. cedonulli* Linnaeus, 1767, on St. Martin; this species is not known north of St. Lucia.]

3. Conus leucostictus Gml
aurantius Brug.

Lamk An s vert Tom XI pag 17 No 12

[Latin description copied from Lamarck.]

Hab. St. Martin & Guadeloupe

4. Conus speciosissimus Reeve
Thesaur Conch Sowb. No 50, fig. 123, 124

[Latin description copied from Sowerby.]

Hab. Curaçao.

[Although Van Rijgersma's water colour clearly shows a specimen of
Conus aurantius, it is doubted is he had collected this shell on
St. Martin or obtained from Guadeloupe.
The species is endemic on the Leeward Islands Curaçao and Bonaire.
Conus speciosissimus Reeve, 1848 was originally described from
Curaçao; it is considered to belong to the species complex of *Conus
magellanicus* Hwass, 1792.
It was not in Van Rijgersma's collection.]

PLATE 45 [*Conus mus* Hwass, 1792]

Groep Obtusely coronated, generally ventricose, short.

5. Conus mus Bruguière

[Latin description copied from Lamarck.]

C. mus Brug. E.M. 27. Lamk. Anim s vert. Tom XI, No 29.
D'Orb. Moll. de Cub. No 296. Thesaur Conch. Spec 57, fig. 78.
Common, all the West Indian Islands.
when the shell has not lost his Epidermis it is of a yellow colour, inside of the mouth blue.

St. Martin
Nov. 1875.

6. Conus barbadensis Brug.

[Latin description copied from Lamarck.]

Habite les mers des Antilles.
Coquille agréable pas sa coloration, et dont la base est un peu granuleuse. long 14 lignes.

[*Conus barbadensis* Hwass, 1792 was named after Barbados, and is considered a junior synonym of *Conus mus*.]

PLATE 46 [*Conus cardinalis* Hwass, 1792]

7. Conus roseus Lamk

Lamk. An s v No 32.

[Latin description copied from Lamarck.]

Habite les mers des Antilles. Ce cone est très distinct du precedent, parce qu'il est silloné transversalement, qu'il n'offre point de lignes colorées, et qu'il est point granuleux inférieusement. la base de sa columelle est tachée de pourpre brun.
longeur 13 lignes et demie.

[The remarks in French are also copied from Lamarck.]

8. Conus cardinalis Lmk.

[Latin description copied from Lamarck.]

Lamk An.s. verteb pag 33.

I have not found nor seen it from St. Martin.

[Van Rijgersma named the figured shell *Conus roseus*, but it is now identified as *Conus cardinalis*, of which he stated that is was unknown to him! The figured specimen probably is not from St. Martin, the species is known from the Greater Antilles and Bahamas.]

PLATE 47   [*Conus jaspideus* Gmelin, 1791]

Groep. Sharp spired with arched outer lip.

9. Conus verrucosus Brug. var.
echinulatus Kiener.
Sowb. Thesaur Conch Conus 80, fig. 125, 127.
[Latin description copied from Sowerby.]
Hab. St. Martin.
2 varieties from my collection, the one nearly smooth the other granulated.
Krebs called this a Conus mindanus Hwass, & Cretaceus, the var b.
Anthony called it C. duvallii Bernardi.

10. Conus centurio Born.
C. tribunus Gml.
[Latin description copied from Sowerby.]
Sowb. Thes. Conch 103, fig. 367
Hab. dans la partie S. des Antilles, les eaux de l'ile Margarita, sur le côte de Venezuela.

[The smooth specimen of the figured shells is presently considered *Conus jaspideus*, whereas the granulated one is the forma *verrucosus* Hwass, 1792 (synonym *echinulatus* Kiener, 1845). It is a common species in the West Indies.
Van Rijgersma did not figure *Conus centurio* Born, 1778, although a specimen from St. Martin was present in his collection (cf. Coomans, 1974: 188).]

PLATE 48 [*Conus daucus* Hwass, 1792]

Groep. Conical not coronated.

11. Conus daucus Brug.
Dict. No 51

[Latin description copied from Lamarck.]

Lmk. anim.s vert. Tom XI pag 47.
D'Orb Moll. de Cuba pag. 114, No 294.
C. arausiacus Chemn.
Sowb. Thesaur. Conch. Spec 142 Fig 188, 189, 330
C. transiensis Chemn X.
St. Martin, not common.

12. Conus coffea Gml.
C. fumigatus Brug. E.M. 94.
[Latin description copied from Lamarck.]
Lamk An.s vert Tome XI page 86
Sowb. Thes. 141, fig 173, 174
Hab. West Indies.

[*Conus daucus* is a well known Antillean species. However, the non-figured *Conus coffeae* is from the Indo-Pacific; its type specimen was recently rediscovered after two centuries, and reported on by Coomans & Visser (1987).]

PLATE 49 [*Conus puncticulatus* Hwass, 1792]

13. Conus columba Brug.
E.M. 101
[Latin description copied from Sowerby.]
Sow Thesaur Spec 156, fig 310, 311
Hab. West Indies

14. Conus pusio Lamk.
C. pygmaeus Reeve.
[Latin description copied from Lamarck.]
Lamk An s v. Tom XI pag 89
Sowb. Thesaur Conch. spec 159, fig 325, 326.
Hab. West Indies, Guadeloupe.

[The two shells on this plate belong to the species complex of *Conus puncticulatus*.
The white shell on top is the colour form *columba* Hwass, 1792.
The lower figure represents the true *C. puncticulatus*, of which *C. pusio* and *C. pygmaeus* are junior synonyms.
The species is confined to the southern Caribbean, the northern limit seems to be Antigua. Therefore Van Rijgersma had no specimens from St. Martin in his collection.]

15. Conus clerii Reeve.
Sowb. Thesaur Conch. 108 fig. 374.
Reeve Z.P. 1843. Conch.Ic. 229.
[Latin description copied from Sowerby.]
Hab. St. Thomas, Brazils.

16. Conus minutus Reeve
Z. Proc. 1843. Conch.Ic. 259
[Latin description copied from Sowerby.]
Sowb. Thesaur. Conch spec 125 fig 360.
Hab. St. Vincents West Indies. Cuming.

Groep. turbinated singular.

17. Conus characteristicus Chemn.
[Latin description copied from Sowerby.]
Sowb. Thesaur Conch. fig 337, 338, spec. 213.
Conus questor and C. muscosus Lmk.
Hab. West Indies, Sowb.
spec. from my collection.

[Van Rijgersma did not figure *Conus clerii* and *C. minutus*, as he had no specimens in his collection. *C. clerii* is from Cape St. Thomas in S. Brazil (not from St. Thomas, Virgin Islands).
C. minutus is a doubtful species.
The figured *C. caracteristicus* Fischer (synonym *C. characteristicus* Dillwyn = Chemnitz) was described from St. Barths, Lesser Antilles. This locality is not correct, since the species is living in the Indo-Pacific. For that reason Van Rijgersma did not mention the locality of the specimen in his collection.]

PLATE 51   [*Conus spurius* cf. *aureofasciatus*]

18. Conus leoninus Brug.
[Latin description copied from Lamarck.]
Lmk. An.sans Vert Tome XI, pag 71
Sowb. Thes. Conch. spec 218, fig 232.
Hab. St. Martin, rare.
Guadeloupe, Schramm.
there appears to be very little difference between this and the following species.
leoninus has a flatter spire and in being rather streaked than spotted the color of the spots is also constantly different.

St. Martin
Nov. 1875.

[The Westindian *Conus spurius* (see plate 52) has a number of colour forms, of which the shell figured here is close to the forma *aureofasciatus* Rehder & Abbott, 1953. It has golden orange to brown bands, instead of the spotted bands of the true *C. spurius*.
C. leoninus Hwass has also a spotted pattern.]

PLATE 52   [*Conus spurius* Gmelin, 1791]

19. Conus spurius Gml.
Conus proteus Brug

[Latin description copied from Lamarck.]

Lmk. An. sans vertr. Tome XI, pag 70
Conus proteus D'Orb. Moll. de Cuba No 297.
Sowb. Thesaur. Conch Spec 220, fig 235, 236.
Hab. St. Thomas W. Indies Sowb.
Cuba & St. Thomas D'Orb.
drawing made from an old specimen out my collection.

20. Conus ochraceus Lmk.
An. s vert Tome XI, pag 67.

[Latin description copied from Sowerby.]

Thes Conch. spec 219.
Loc. West Indies.

[Van Rijgersma had no figure of *Conus ochraceus* Lamarck, 1810. It is considered another colour form of *C. spurius* in which the spots have fused into large irregular areas, of an ochre colour.]

PLATE 53   [*Conus ermineus* Born, 1778]

21. Conus testudinarius Martini
[Latin description copied from Lamarck.]
Lmk. An sans vert. XI, page 77.
var b. testa aurantia, albo variegata.
Hab. from Guadeloupe Coll: Marie.

22. Conus Porto-ricanus Brug.
[Latin description copied from Lamarck.]
Lmk. An s.V. pag. 95, Spec 135.
Habite les Mers des Antilles, sur les côtes de Porto-Rico.
Sowb. Thesaur. Conch 237 fig. 433.

23. Conus Narcissus Lmk
An. s v Tom XI p. 80
[Latin description copied from Lamarck.]
Sowb. Thesaur Conus spec. 240 fig. 436.
Hab. West Indies.

[*Conus ermineus* is the first name for a species which was known for a long time as *Conus testudinarius* Hwass, 1792. Van Rijgersma also figured a specimen with a golden colour, which he called the variety b, 'aurantia'.
The two other names on this plate, *Conus portoricanus* Hwass, 1792, and *C. narcissus* Lamarck, 1810, are junior synonyms of *Conus ermineus*.]

PLATE 54   [*Conus granulatus* Linné, 1758]

24. Conus mercator Linn.
C. reticulatus Mart.
Syst. Nat. ed 12, pag 1169.
[Latin description copied from Lamarck.]
Lmk An. s vert Tom XI p 66.
Sowb. Thesaur conch. spec 253 fig 294, 295.
Hab. West Indies.

Groep. Narrow, cylindrical, spire rounded with close perpendicular whorls.

25. Conus granulatus Linn.
[Latin description copied from Lamarck.]
Lamk. An s v. Tom XI, page 101.
Sowb Thesaur Conch Spec 92, fig 540, 541.
Hab. Guadeloupe, Schramm.
Antigua & St. Kitts, Dr. Branch.
Semifossil species from Barbados.

[*Conus mercator* Linnaeus, 1758, was not present in Van Rijgersma's collection. This species is living on the coast of West Africa, it is not known from the West Indies.
The figured *Conus granulatus* is a rare Caribbean species, not found by Van Rijgersma on St. Martin. Since the figured specimen is not coloured red, it is probably the semifossil shell from Barbados.]

25. Conus Mazei Deshayes.
C. Mazei Deshayes. Journal de Conch 1874, pag 64.
[Latin description copied from Deshayes.]
Hab. Martinique. Coll. H. Mazé
this shell is at present unique.

St. Martin, 1875.

[This species was named after Van Rijgersma's friend Hippolyte Mazé from Guadeloupe (see p. 29). He must have received a reprint of the publication, from which he copied the two figures on this plate. It was the last *Conus* species in his manuscript, which was followed by an index of the Conidae.]

List of W. Indian Cones.

Conus armillatus C. B. Adams
   (Contrib. No 4, page 59.)
Conus aurantius Brug.
   = leucostictus Gml.
Conus Barbadensis Brug.
Conus cedo-nulli Linn.
Conus centurio Born
Conus characteristicus Chemn.
   = questor & muscosus Lmk
Conus columba Brug.
Conus cretaceus (Mindanus var.)
Conus daucus
Conus echinulatus Kiener
   var. of verrucosus
Conus fumigatus = coffea
Conus granulatus Linn.
Conus leoninus.

Conus leucostictus = aurantius
Conus mercator
Conus minutus Reeve
Conus mus
Conus nebulosus
Conus nodiferus
Conus Porto-ricanus
Conus punctatus – piperatus
   = biliosus
Conus purpurascens
Conus pusio = pygmaeus
Conus radiatus
Conus roseus
Conus spurius
Conus testudinarius
Conus varius
Conus villepini

[The family Conidae is being studied at the Department of Malacology, Zoological Museum Amsterdam. An alphabetical revision is published in the journal 'Basteria' (vols. 43-50, 1979-1986, contin.) by H. E. Coomans, R. G. Moolenbeek & E. Wils. Special topics are discussed in the series 'Studies on Conidae' (nos. 1-14, 1982-1988) published by the same Department.]

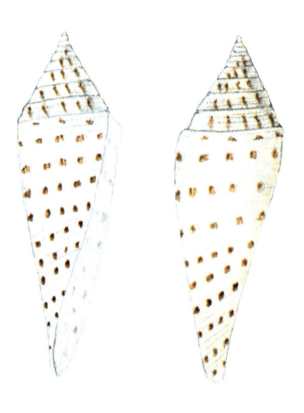

Family Turridae

Pleurotoma affinis
[Latin description copied from Reeve.]
Hab. Isl. of St. Vincent W. I. Guilding.
Magnified to twice its natural length.

Pleurotoma cancellata (Gray)
Reeve Monogr. Spec 317, pl. XXXV.
[Latin description copied from Reeve.]
Hab. Isl. of St. Vincent: Guilding.

[Van Rijgersma figured six specimens of the Turridae in his manuscript, all placed in the genus *Pleurotoma*. On this plate are combined *Crassispira affinis* (Reeve, 1846) on top, and *Crassispira cancellata* (Reeve, 1846). He did not state if they were collected on St. Martin.
In addition to the six figured species he mentioned the following twelve species, only with name, author and reference:
Pleurotoma albella C. B. Adams. Contrib. pag. 63. Hab. Jamaica.
Pleur. albida C. B. Adams. Synopsis Conch. Jamaicensium pag 3.
Pleur. alabaster Reeve. Plate VIII Spec. 65. Said to be from Cartagena.
Pleur. albocincta C. B. Adams. Synop. Conch Jamaic. pag 3.
Pleur. albo-maculata C. B. Adams. Syn. Conch Jamaic. pag 3.
Pleur. albo-maculata D'Orb. Moll de Cuba pag. 1 pl. XXIV fig. 16, 18.
Pleur. Antillarum D'Orb. Moll de Cuba pag. 173 pl XXIV fig. 1, 3.
Pleur. angustae C. B. Ad. Contrib. to Conch. pag 61. Hab. Jamaica.
Pleur. Auberianae D'Orb. Moll de Cuba pag. 174 pl. XXIV f.7, 3, 9.
Pleur. balteata Reeve. Hab. St. Thomas.
Pleur. Candeana D'Orb. Moll de Cuba pag 175 pl. XXIV, fig. X, XII.
Pleur. Caribaea D'Orb. Moll de Cuba.]

Pleurotoma angulifera Reeve
Reeve Conch. Icon. vol. I plate XXXIX spec. 360.
[Latin description copied from Reeve.]
Hab. West Indies. highly magnified.

Pleurotoma coccinata Reeve.
[Latin description copied from Reeve.]
Monogr. Plate XXXIII, spec. 299.
magnified 3 times.

[On this plate are combined *Tenaturris angulifera* (Reeve, 1846) above, and *Cerodrillia coccinata* (Reeve, 1845) below. Van Rijgersma did not mention if the shells were collected on St. Martin, or obtained by exchange. Both are Westindian species.]

[*Daphnella candidula & clathrata*] PLATE 58

Pleurotoma candidula Reeve
Conch. Icon. vol. I, pl. XXXIX Spec. 358
[Latin description copied from Reeve.]
Hab. West Indies (d'Orb).
Highly magnified.

Pleurotoma clathrata Reeve.
Monogr. pl. XXXIV spec. 361.
[Latin description copied from Reeve.]
Hab. West Indies D'Orb.
highly magnified.

[The two species of this plate are now identified as *Daphnella cancellata* (Reeve, 1846) above, and *Daphnella clathrata* (Reeve, 1846) below. Also with these two turrids Van Rijgersma did not state the locality of his specimens.]

152   PLATE 59   [*Pleurobranchus quadridens* (Mörch, 1863)]

Family Pleurobranchidae

Genus Berthella, Blainville.

Berthella quadridens Mörch.
[Latin description copied from Mörch.]
Mörch Contributions.
long 5 mill. lat 3 mill.
Hab. St. Martin.
St. Thomas. Guadeloupe.

[Van Rijgersma had included two specimens from the subclass of the Opisthobranchia in his manuscript. He placed them both in the family Pleurobranchidae.
The crawling animal of *Pleurobranchus quadridens* was figured from several aspects.]

PLATE 60 [*Dolabrifera ascifera* (Rang, 1828)]

Dolabrifera
Shell trapezoidal;
side lobes not used for swimming.

Dolabrifera ascifera Rang
loc. St. Martin St. Barthelemew. not rare
St. Thomas et S. Croix. Tres-commun (Riise et Oersted).
Guadeloupe (Schramm).

[The genus *Dolabrifera* is now placed in the family Aplysiidae. Van Rijgersma made a drawing of the crawling animal, and two figures of the small shell, which is internal in the seaslugs.]

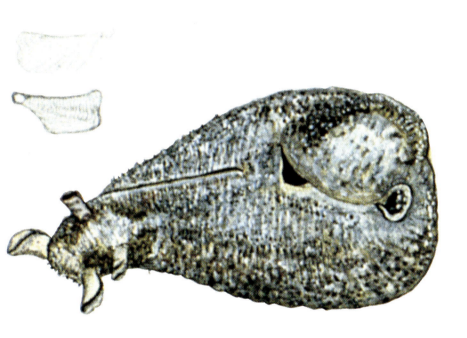

Family Auriculidae [= Ellobiidae]

Amphibious animals living at the sea shore on sticks, under seaweed, or at the roots of the mangrove trees (Rhizophora mangle).

Genus Melampus.

Melampus coffeus Linn.
Voluta minuta Gml. Syst. nat.
Ellobium Barbadense Bolt. doc Pfr
Bulimus coniformis Brug. Dict no 72.
[Latin description copied from Lamarck.]
Hab. Antilles, Florida very common
St. Martin Simsonbaylagoon on sticks.

Melampus flavus Gme
[Latin description copied from Lamarck.]
Auricula monilis Lmk. An s.V.Tom VIII, pag 333.
M. coronatus C. B. Adams. Contrib pag 41.
M. coronulus H & A. Ad.

Obconic smooth, Spire short, convex, suture slightly impressed, whorls 9-10, aperture narrow, lip with about ten transverse ribs within, parietal wall and columella each with a prominent fold. Chestnut color, with three equidistant revolving light colored bands.
Length 13, diam 8.6 mill.
Hab. Florida. From West Indies. (Tryon), not common
under seaweed, St. Martin.
Tab XIII fig. 4-7 from Ramon de la Sagra, Atlas, is Mel. flavus, fig. 5-6 M. coffeus & 1-3 M. pusillus. –

[With *Melampus coffeus* (Linnaeus, 1758), Van Rijgersma made two colour drawings of the shell, and figures of the head and the crawling animal from the underside.
Melampus flavus is now identified as *Pira monile* (Bruguière, 1789).]

158   PLATE 62   [*Tralia ovula* (Bruguière, 1789)]

Melampus pusillus Gml
Bulimus ovulus Brug.
Auricula nitens Lmk.
Voluta triplicata Donov. doc. Pfr.
[Latin description copied from d'Orbigny.]
D'Orb Moll de Cuba pag 137.
Hab. St. Martin under seaweed on the bayside.
West Indies & Florida.
Whorls 6-7, the last slightly shouldered;
aperture narrow above, much wider below, lip simple, acute, with a transverse lamina within, columella with a prominent fold, parietal wall with two teeth.
Color dark brown and leaden. the longest measure 15 mill but mostly smaller, by the young animal (which I had occasion to examin) was the foot divided tranversely.

[This species is now identified as *Tralia ovula*. Next to the colour drawings of the shell, Van Rijgersma made two figures of the crawling animal, and the underside of the animal.]

PLATE 63   [*Detracia bullaoides* (Montagu, 1808)]

Melampus cingulatus Pfeiffer.
Auricula oliva D'Orb.
[Latin description copied from d'Orbigny.]
Hab. West Indies and Florida.
St. Martin, rare.

[At present this species is called *Detracia bullaoides*.]

PLATE 64   [*Pedipes mirabilis* (Mühlfeld, 1818)]

Genus Pedipes Adanson

Subglobose, imperforate, transversely striate, spire short; aperture narrow, parietal wall concave with three plaits, of which the posterior is largest, outer lip with a sinus behind. two internal teeth, and an acute margin. Foot divided below by a transverse groove.

Pedipes mirabilis Muhlf.
Pedipes quadridens Pfr in Wiegm Arch 1839, p. 357.
P. tridens Pfr in Proc. Zool. Soc. 1854, p. 122.
P. ovalis C. B. Adams. Contrib. to Conch page 41.

Hab. Habana (Arango). Guadeloupe, Barbados, St. Martin. On the seashore under stones, seaweed & where the influende of fresh water can be felt. Animal much smaller than these of the neighbouring Islands, the largest and most perfect I have from Barbados, of which locality I have coppied one.
Animal (by the St. Martin Spec. considered young ones) transparent white, feelers, eyes & mouth black with 2 broad frontal lobes, feet divided across.
Not walking like Truncatella, but sliding like a common snail.
Measure spec. from Barbados length 6 millm by 4.5 mm.
Spec. from St. Martin length 2.5 by 2 millm.

[Also with this species Van Rijgersma figured the shell; and in pencil a crawling animal seen from the underside, and from above.]

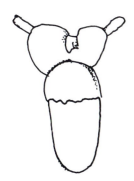
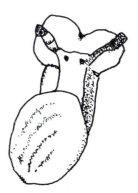

PLATE 65 [*Trachycardium isocardia* (Linné, 1758)]

Family Cardiidae

Genus Cardium Linn. Subgenus Trachycardium Mörch.

Cardium isocardia Linn. SystNat
Lamk. An sans vert Tom VI, Spec 17
D'Orb. Moll de Cub pag 307 No 512.

[Latin description copied from d'Orbigny.]

Diam. 80 mill.

St. Martin, Simsonbay in het zand, niet zeldzaam.
Guadeloupe Schramm. Cuba, St. Lucie, Martinique D'Orb.
het is een van de groote soorten ofschoon er ook een kleinder soort gevonden word met een paar meer ribben en ronder, ribben niet altijd 35 soms een paar minder of meer.
van binnen is de schelp prachtig rose rood van af de spitsen tot half verwege, verder witachtig
grootste soort, hoogte 65 millemeter
omtrek 150 mil.m.
klein exempl. hoogte 23 millm
omtrek 70 mill.

[St. Martin, Simson Bay in sand, not rare. Guadeloupe Schramm. Cuba, St. Lucia, Martinique D'Orb. It is one of the larger species although also a smaller species is found with more ribs and more roundish. Ribs not always 35 sometimes a few less or more, the inside of the shell is beautifully rose red from the apex to half way down, further whitish. Large specimen, length 65 mm, outline 150 mm; small specimen: length 23 mm, outline 70 mm.

This is the only pelecypod family which was treated by Van Rijgersma in his manuscript on the molluscs of St. Martin. Most of the speceis were described in Dutch. For all species he used the generic name *Cardium*.]

PLATE 66 [*Trachycardium muricatum* (Linné, 1758)]

Cardium muricatum L.
Cardium muricatum Linn. Syst. Nat.
Card. Campechiense Bolten. Mus 191
Lamk. An sans vert No 18
D'Orb. Moll de Cub pag 305 No 507

[Latin description copied from d'Orbigny.]

localiteit. St. Martin Simsonbaij, Matacorda bay Texas & Brasilie. in mijne verzameling. St. Thomas (Swift) Cuba. Martinique Guadeloupe & Jamaica (D'Orb.) niet zeldzaam, maar nog al in kleur verschillende, sommigen zijn geheel wit en de dubbele langwerpige purper geele streep in de schep bestaat niet; de gewone met bruine vlekken, en met orange vlekken de 2 strepen inwendig ook orange geel.
een groot voorwerp hoog 50 mill. Breedte 45 millm.
ribben meest 35.
Met Cardium senticosum Sowb. van Panama heeft het zeer veel overeenkomst.

[locality, St. Martin Simson Bay, Matacorda Bay Texas & Brazil, in my collection. St. Thomas (Swift) Cuba, Martinique, Guadeloupe & Jamaica (d'Orb.) not rare, but variable in colour, some are totally white and the double elongate purplish yellow stripe within the shell is not present; the ordinary with brown spots, and with orange spots the 2 stripes internally also orange yellow, a large specimen length 50 mm, width 45 mm, ribs mostly 35. The species looks very much like *Cardium senticosum* Sowb. from Panama.]

168 PLATE 67 [*Trachycardium magnum* (Linné, 1758)]

Cardium subelongatum Sowb.
Cardium angulatum D'Orb Moll de Cuba No 510.

[Latin description copied from d'Orbigny.]

Diam. 40 mill.

Deze schelp is gemakkelijk te herkennen van isocardia & muricata, door zijn langwerpige vorm en omdat het slechts zeer weinig en dan wel alleen bij de rand gestekeld is. Goede exemplaren zijn geheel met een vrij dikke geel opperhuid bedekt, van binnen geheel wit behalve de achterrand die schoon citroengeel is, slotgroeven geelachtig en de gekartelde rand steenrood. De naam C. angulatum Lmk An. s. v. Tom VI, no. 19 bl. 399 wordt meestal niet gebruikt, omdat, la coquille qui, dans la collection du Museum, port ce nom, est un grand et bel individu du Card. rugosum no 23. Hoogte van mijn grootste exempl. 70 millm. breedte 55 millm. dikte 40 millm.

[This shell is easily to be distinguished from *isocardia & muricata* by its elongate shape and because it has very few spines and only at the sides. Fine specimens are covered completely with a rather thick yellow epidermis, inside white except the posterior margin which is nice lemon yellow, hinge grooves yellowish, and the notched margin stony red. The name *C. angulatum* Lmk. Anim. sans Vert., vol. 6, no. 19, p. 399 is mostly not used, because the shell in the collection of the Museum which bears this name is a large and nice specimen of *Card. rugosum* no. 23. Length of my largest specimen 70 mm, width 55 mm, thick 40 mm.]

PLATE 68   [*Papyridea hiatus* & *P. semisulcata*]

Genus Papyridea Swainson.
De achterkant gezaagd. Schelp zeer dun.
[The backside sawed. Shell very thin.]

Cardium bullatum Linn.
Cardium bullatum Lmk. C. soleniforme Brug.
C. spinosum Meuschen.
C. aspersum Sowb. Zool. Proc. 1833.
[Latin description copied from d'Orbigny.]
loc. St. Martin, in het zand Simsonbay. West Indies. Varieert in kleur en heeft op iedere klep 45-50 dunne ribben, dus veel minder dan het voorwerp door D'Orb. beschreven.

Cardium ringiculum Sow. Zool. Proc 1840
Cardium Petitianum D'Orb. Mol. de Cuba
[Latin description copied from d'Orbigny.]
diam. 18 mill.
loc. St. Martin, niet zeldzaam, en verscheidene andere eilanden St. Thomas, Guadeloupe, Cuba Martinique etc. Varieert in kleuren waarvan de voornaamste zijn wit met rood aan de spitsen, geheel citroengeel of orange, heeft veel overeenkomst met bullatum en is misschien wel een jong van bovengenoemd weekdier, temeer nog daar ik nooit geen kleine voorwerpen van Bullatum gezien heb.

[Van Rijgersma discussed two species on this plate. The one above is *Papyridea hiatus* (Meuschen, 1787).
loc. St. Martin, in sand, Simson Bay. West Indies. Colour variable and on each valve has 45-50 thin ribs, thus less than the specimen described by d'Orbigny.
The figure below is not a juvenile shell, but a distinct species: *Papyridea semisulcata* (Gray, 1825).
loc. St. Martin, not rare, and some other islands St. Thomas, Guadeloupe, Cuba, Martinique etc. Variable in colour, the main colours are white with red at the apex, lemon yellow all over or orange, looks much like *bullatum* and is perhaps a juvenile of that mollusc, especially since I have never seen small specimens of *bullatum*.]

PLATE 69 [*Laevicardium laevigatum* (Linné, 1758)]

Genus Liocardium Mörch
schelp langwerpig ovaal, ongelijkzijdig, oppervlakte der kleppen eenvoudig zonder rubben of doornen, slecht weinig gapende.

Cardium serratum Linn.
Cardium laevigatum Gml. Syst. Nat. 3251.
Cardium Citrinum Chemn.
Cardium oviputamen Reeve.?
[Latin description copied from d'Orbigny.]
long. 42 Millm.
St. Martin in het zand niet zeldzaam.
Guadeloupe, St. Thomas & Barbados enz.
aux côtes du Bresil et des Antilles: D'Orb.
drie verscheidenheden bestaan van deze schelp
1. de hier afgebeelde Citroengeel van kleur.
2. wit met bruine ziczac vlekken of streepjes.
3. Orange geel met dunne concentrische streepjes, ook verschilt veel in groote –

Cardium glabratum Roemer. Chemn.
Cardium laevigatum Linné
vide D'Orb Moll de Cub No 509. Long 74 millm.
[Latin description copied from d'Orbigny.]
Wordt hier niet gevonden, en schijnt zeldzaam te zijn.
Eiland Marguerite D'Orb. St. Thomas (Swift).

[It seems that Van Rijgersma was confused about the nomenclature of the species names on this plate. The figured shell is *Laevicardium laevigatum* (Linnaeus, 1758). He remarked:
loc. St. Martin in sand not rare, Guadeloupe, St. Thomas & Barbados etc. the coasts of Brazil and the Antilles: d'Orb.
There are three varieties of this shell: 1. the one here figured lemon yellow in colour, 2. white with brown ziczac spots or stripes, 3. orange yellow with thin concentric stripes. Also the size is variable.
With *C. glabratum* he said: 'is not found here, and seems to be rare'.]

PLATE 70 [*Americardia antillarum* (d'Orbigny, 1846)]

Cardium Antillarum D'Orb. 1846
Cardium graniferum Sowb et Brod. 1844.
[Latin description copied from d'Orbigny.]
Diam. 7 millm.
if our Shell is the C. graniferum of Brod & Sowb found at the Pacific coast of Central America his name should be retained as it has two years precedence. I have not seen the pacific shell but it appears to me Dr. Carpenter thinks them to be different as he don't quote our shell, and sais of his Mazatlan species 'The interstices between the ribs are decussated by a series of rectangular impressed pits laid transversely', while D'Orb. diagnosis is 'interstitiis transversum striatis'.
Not found at St. Martin.
Cuba, Guadeloupe, Martinique, Jamaica D'Orb.
St. Thomas (R. Swift).

[This very small species was not found by Van Rijgersma at St. Martin. The present author has collected the related *Americardia guppyi* (Thiele, 1910) on the coast of French St. Martin.]

PLATE 71 [*Hemicardia media* (Linné, 1758)]

Genus Hemicardia Klein.

Cardium Medium Linn.
Cardium medium D'Orb. Moll de Cuba No 511.
[Latin description copied from d'Orbigny.]
diam 40 mill.
Zeer algemeen over de West Indies verbreidt,
et sur la cotes des Florides. D'Orb.

[Very common in the West Indies,
and at the coast of Florida, d'Orbigny.]

[At the end of the family Van Rijgersma gave a list of species:]

West Indian Cardiums
C. Antillarum D'Orb = Hemicardia granifera Brod.
C. Citrinum Chem. = serratum Linn Liocardium
C. Isocardia Linn.
C. laevigatum Linn. = Liocardium glabratum Roemer
C. leucostomum Born = Marmoreum Lamk. loc. Singapoore
C. medium Linn.
C. muricatum Linn. = C. Campechiense Bolten
C. oviputamen Reeve = Liocardium serratum ?
C. pictum Dunker Antilles ?
C. petitianum D'Orb = Papyridea ringicula Sowb.
C. Spinosum Meuschen = bullata Linn.
C. subelongatum Sowb. = C. angulatum Lmk.
C. Hemicardia venusta Dunker Antilles ?
Verticordia, vel Trigonulina ornata D'Orb.

PLATE 72   [*Verticordia ornata* (d'Orbigny, 1842)]

[Family Verticordiidae]

Genus Verticordia S. Wood

Shell suborbicular with radiating ribs, beaks sub. spiral; margins denticulated; interior brilliantly pearly; right valve with 1 prominent cardinal tooth; adductor scars 2, faint; pallial line simple; ligament internal, oblique; epidermis dark brown. Woodwards Manual fol. 472.

Trigonulina ornata D'Orb: Jamaica.
has hinge teeth 2.2. right valve with a long posterior tooth; Epidermis of large nucleated cells, as in Trigoniadae, to which family it undoubtedly belong.
[Latin description copied from d'Orbigny.]
Diam 2 mill.
Not found in St. Martin,
shell copied from the Moll de Cuba.

[Although Van Rijgersma included this species with the Cardiidae, he realized that *Verticordia* belongs to a separate family. Presently it is placed in the family Verticordiidae.]

[*Dentalium semistriatum & antillarum*]

Klasse Scaphopoda. Bronn. Scaufelfüsser.

Family Dentaliidae
Shell tubular.

Genus Dentalium
Dentalium translucidum Desh.
[Latin description copied from Sowerby.]
Th. Conch. Sowb. vol III pag 98, No 7 fig 47.
Lmk. An s vert. Tome V, pag 597 No 176.
D. semistriatum Guilding. name praeoccupied for a fossil species.
Most of the specimen are not light yellow or ambre colored but pure white. When the shells become older and more solid the fissure at the apex disappears and nearby half of the shell becomes finely striated. Those may be called the var. *semistriatum* Guilding.
While others gradually become wholy striated with the apex ribbed the var. *Antillarum* D'Orb. Moll de Cub No 409.
Some again as is the case with the European D. entalis, are entirely ribbed and beautifully marked with transparent squarish spots on the ribs, may not these constitute I believe an other var. the
Dent. disparile D'Orb. Moll. de Cuba, spec 406.
loc. St. Martin and other W. Indian Islands, not common.
St. Thomas, Martinique, D'Orb.
Guadeloupe (Schramm).

Dentalium Antillarum D'Orb.
[Latin description copied from d'Orbigny.]

[The family Dentaliidae have large shells, with the shape of an elephant tusk. The two species on this plate are: *Dentalium semistriatum* Turton, 1819, on top, and *D. antillarum* d'Orbigny, 1842, below.]

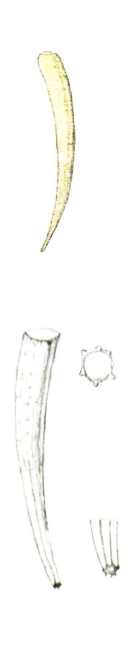

PLATE 74   [*Dentalium disparile* & *Cadulus dominguensis*]

Dentalium disparile D'Orb. No 410.
[Latin description copied from d'Orbigny.]
Moll. de Cuba part sec. pag. 202

[Family Siphonodentaliidae]

Dentalium Dominguense D'Orb.
[Latin description copied from d'Orbigny.]
D'Orb Moll. de Cuba 1846 No 408, Pl XXV Fig. 7-9.
St. Domingo, Martinique, Guadeloupe, St. Thomas, Cuba, D'Orb.
St. Martin mixed with small shells on the seabeach.

[The species on top is *Dentalium disparile* d'Orbigny, 1842.
Van Rijgersma did not mention if the specimen was from St. Martin.
The species below was placed by him in the genus *Dentalium*,
presently it is identified as *Cadulus dominguensis* (d'Orbigny, 1842) of
the family Siphonodentaliidae. These are small shells with the widest
part in the middle.]

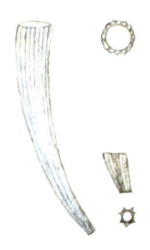

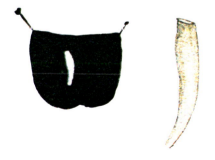

LITERATURE

ADAM, W., 1937. Céphalopodes des îles Bonaire et Curaçao. Capita Zoologica 8(3), p. 1-29.
BAKER, H. BURRINGTON, 1924. New land operculates from the Dutch Leeward Islands. Nautilus 37, p. 89-94.
—, 1924. Land and freshwater Molluscs of the Dutch Leeward Islands. Occ. Pap. Mus. Zool. Michigan 152, p. 1-159.
—, 1925. Isolation and Curaçao. Nautilus 39, p. 40-44.
BENTHEM JUTTING, W. S. S. VAN, 1925. On a collection of non-marine Mollusca from Curaçao. Bijdr. Dierk. 24, p. 25-32.
—, 1927. Marine molluscs of the island of Curaçao. Bijdr. Dierk. 25, p. 1-36.
BINNEY, W. G., 1884. Notes on the jaw and lingual dentition of pulmonate mollusks. Ann. N.Y. Acad. Sci. 3, p. 79-136.
BOEKE, J., 1907. Rapport betreffende een voorlopig onderzoek naar den toestand van de visscherij en de industrie van zeeproducten in de kolonie Curaçao. 1. 's-Gravenhage.
BOERSTRA, E. H. J., 1982. De precolumbiaanse bewoners van Aruba, Curaçao en Bonaire. Zutphen, 79 p.
BLAND, TH., 1871. Notes relating to the physical geography and geology of, and the distribution of terrestrial Mollusca in certain West India islands. Proc. Am. phil. Soc. 12, p. 56-63.
BLAND, TH. & W. G. BINNEY, 1871. Notes on the genus Pineria. Ann. Lyc. nat. Hist. 10, p. 22-27.
BREURE, A. S. H., 1974. Caribbean land molluscs: Bulimulidae. I. Bulimulus. Stud. Fauna Curaçao 45, p. 1-80.
BRUGGEMAN-NANNENGA, M. A. & P. WAGENAAR HUMMELINCK, 1986. Notes on the Caribbean crown conch Melongena melongena. Stud. Fauna Curaçao 68, p. 148-190.
BUISONJÉ, P. H. DE, 1974. Neogene and Quaternary Geology of Aruba, Curaçao and Bonaire. 293 p. (Thesis Univ. Amsterdam.)
CLENCH, W. J., 1970. Land Mollusca of Saba island, Lesser Antilles. Occ. Pap. Moll. 3, p. 53-60.
COOMANS, H. E., 1958. A survey of the littoral Gastropoda of the Netherlands Antilles. Stud. Fauna Curaçao 8, p. 42-111.
—, 1959. Rapport betreffende het economisch gebruik van weekdieren van de Nederlandse Antillen. Curaçao, 60 p.
—, 1963. The marine Mollusca of St. Martin, Lesser Antilles, collected by H. J. Krebs. Stud. Fauna Curaçao 16, p. 59-87.
—, 1963. The marine Mollusca of St. Martin, Lesser Antilles, especially from the French part. J. Conchyl. Paris 103, p. 113-186.
—, 1963. Systematics and distribution of Siphocypraea mus and Propustularia surinamensis. Stud. Fauna Curaçao 15, p. 51-71.
—, 1964. De eerste schelpenfauna van Curaçao, in Simons' beschrijving van dit eiland. Nwe. West-Ind. Gids 43, p. 195-210.
—, 1965. Teralatirus, a new genus in the Fasciolariidae. Basteria 29, p. 10-14.
—, 1967. The classification of Columbella dormitor with the description of a new genus Minipyrene. Beaufortia 14, p. 71-80.

—, 1967. The non-marine Mollusca of St. Martin. Stud. Fauna Curaçao 24, p. 118-145.
—, 1970. Volksnamen voor weekdieren op de Nederlandse Antillen. Nwe West-Ind. Gids 47, p. 158-186.
—, 1972. The genus Pachybathron. Basteria 36, p. 89-96.
—, 1973. Additional notes on the genus Pachybathron. Argamon 4, p. 11-14.
—, 1973. H. E. van Rijgersma, gouvernementsarts op St. Maarten, 1863-1877. In: L. W. Statius van Eps & E. Luckman-Maduro, Van scheepschirurgijn tot specialist. Assen, p. 13-17.
—, 1974. Life and malacological work of Hendrik Elingsz van Rijgersma (1835-1877). Bijdr. Dierk. 44, p. 115-214. (Thesis Univ. Amsterdam.)
—, 1987. Shell objects from Indian sites at Curaçao, Bonaire and Aruba. UNA Uitgave 31, p. 6-14.
—, 1988. The distribution of Cypraea surinamensis with remarks on its rarity, taxonomy and shell dimorphism. In: Stud. honour P. Wagenaar Hummelinck. Amsterdam, p. 199-207.
COOMANS H. E. & M. COOMANS-EUSTATIA, 1988. Flowers from St. Martin, the 19th century watercolours of westindian plants painted by Hendrik van Rijgersma. Zutphen, 160 p.
COOMANS, H. E. & F. F. J. M. PIETERS, 1985. On the discovery of portraits of G. B. Sowerby II and III, and letters of G. B. Sowerby III to H. E. van Rijgersma. Archiv. nat. Hist. 12, p. 135-142.
COOMANS H. E. & J. S. DE VISSER, 1987. Studies on Conidae, 10. The holotype and identity of Conus coffeae Gmelin. Veliger 29, p. 437-441.
CROSSE, H. & TH. BLAND, 1873. Description de mollusques nouveaux provenant de Curaçao et de Sainte-Lucie. J. Conchyl. Paris 21, p. 40-44.
EMANUELS, B. J., 1933. Iets over Bilharzia op de Boven-windsche eilanden. Geneesk. Tijdschr. Ned.-Indië 73, p. 286-288.
ENGEL, H., 1925. Westindische Opisthobranchiate Mollusken. Bijdr. Dierk. 24, p. 33-80. (Thesis Univ. Amsterdam.)
—, 1927. Westindische Opisthobranchiate Mollusken, II. Bijdr. Dierk. 25, p. 83-122.
ENGEL, H. & P. WAGENAAR HUMMELINCK, 1936. Ueber Westindische Aplysiidae und Verwandten anderer Gebiete. Capita Zool. 8, p. 1-76.
EUWENS, P. A., 1923. De paarlvisscherij bij het eiland Margarita. West-Ind. Gids 41, p. 513-532.
GLASSCOCK, J., 1985. The making of an island: Sint Maarten-Saint Martin. Massachusetts, 180 p.
GOULD, S., 1969. Character variation in two land snails from the Dutch Leeward islands; geography, environment and evolution. Syst. Zool. 18, p. 185-200.
—, 1971. The paleontological evolution of Cerion 2: age and fauna of Indian shell middens on Curaçao and Aruba. Breviora 372, p. 1-26.
—, 1984. Covariance sets and ordered geographic variation in Cerion from Aruba, Bonaire and Curaçao, a way of studying nonadaptation. Syst. Zool. 33, p. 217-237.
GIJZEN, A., 1938. 's Rijksmuseum van Natuurlijke Historie 1820-1915. Rotterdam, 335 p. (Thesis Univ. Leiden.)
HAAS, F., 1960. Caribbean land molluscs: Vertiginidae. Stud. Fauna Curaçao 10, p. 1-18.
—, 1962. Caribbean land molluscs: Subulinidae and Oleacinidae. Stud. Fauna Curaçao 13, p. 49-60.

HAVISER, J. B., 1987. Amerindian cultural geography on Curaçao. Amsterdam, 212 p. (Thesis Univ. Leiden.)
HEEKEREN, H. R. VAN, 1960. A survey of the non ceramic artefacts of Aruba, Curaçao and Bonaire. Nwe. West-Ind. Gids 40, p. 103-120.
HOLTHUIS, L. B., 1959. H. E. van Rijgersma, a littleknown naturalist of St. Martin (Netherlands Antilles). Stud. Fauna Curaçao 9, p. 69-78.
—, 1961. Nadere gegevens betreffende H. E. van Rijgersma. Nwe. West-Ind. Gids 41, p. 166-167.
HORST, R. & M. M. SCHEPMAN, 1894-1908. Cataloque systématique des mollusques. Mus. Hist. nat. Pays Bas 13 (1-3), 572 p.
HOVESTADT, A., 1987. De landslakken van Aruba, Curaçao en Bonaire. Corr. blad Ned. Mal. Ver. 235, p. 245-252.
JONG, K. M. DE & H. E. COOMANS, 1988. Marine gastropods from Curaçao, Aruba and Bonaire. Leiden, 261 p.
JONG, K. M. DE & I. KRISTENSEN, 1965. Gegevens over mariene gastropoden van Curaçao. Corr. blad Ned. Mal. Ver., suppl. 1965, 56 p.
—, 1968. Gegevens over de Mollusken van Curaçao uitgezonderd de mariene gastropoden. Corr. blad Ned. Mal. Ver., suppl. 1968, 46 p.
JUNG, P., 1974. Eocene Mollusks from Curaçao, West Indies. Verhandl. Naturf. Ges. Basel 84, p. 483-500.
KAAS, P., 1972. Polyplacophora of the Caribbean region. Stud. Fauna Curaçao 41, p. 1-162.
KOOLWIJK, A. J. VAN, 1884. Parelvisscherij op Aruba. Tijdschr. Ned. Aardr. Gen. (2) 1, p. 601-602.
KREBS, H. J., 1864. The West-Indian marine shells with some remarks. Nykjobing, 37 p.
KRISTENSEN, I., 1965. Habitat of the tidal gastropod Echininus nodulosus. Basteria 29, p. 23-25.
KUYP, E. VAN DER, 1949. Planorbidae records of the Netherlands Antilles. Amer. J. Trop. Med. 29, p. 259-261.
—, Notes on the Planorbidae in the Netherlands Antilles. Quat. J. Trop. Med. Hyg. 3, p. 283-284.
LORIÉ, J., 1887. Fossile Mollusken von Curaçao, Aruba und der Küste von Venezuela. Samml. Geol. Reichsmus. Leiden 2 (1), p. 111-149.
MARCUS DU BOIS REYMOND, E. & E. MARCUS, 1963. Opisthobranchs from the Lesser Antilles. Stud. Fauna Curaçao 19, p. 1-77.
MARCUS, E. & E. DU BOIS REYMOND-MARCUS, 1970. Opisthobranchs from Curaçao and faunistically related regions. Stud. Fauna Curaçao 33, p. 1-129.
MAZÉ, H., 1890. Supplément au catalogue révisé des mollusques terrestres et fluviatiles de la Guadeloupe et de ses dépendances. J. Conchyl. Paris 31, p. 5-54.
MELVILL, J. C., 1891. A new species of Latirus. Notes Leyden Mus. 13, p. 158.
MÖRCH, O. A. L., 1875-1877. Synopsis Molluscorum Marinorum Indiarum occidentalium. Malakozool. Bl. 22-24.
MOOLENBEEK, R. G., 1984. Pickfordiateuthis pulchella (Cephalopoda: Myopsida): range extension to Bonaire. Stud. Fauna Curaçao 67, p. 104-109.
MOOLENBEEK, R. G. & M. J. FABER, 1984. A new gastropod genus and species from Bonaire, Netherlands Antilles. Stud. Fauna Curaçao 67, p. 98-103.
—, 1988. The genus Euchelus (Prosobranchia: Trochidae) in the West Indies. In: Stud. honour P. Wagenaar Hummelinck. Amsterdam, p. 217-226.

NIERSTRASZ, H. F., 1927. Chitonida. Bijdrage tot de kennis der fauna van Curaçao. Bijdr. Dierk. 25, p. 162-163.

PADDENBURG, G. G. VAN, 1819. Beschrijving van het eiland Curaçao en onderhoorige eilanden. Haarlem, 90 p.

PEL, P. L. VAN, 1969. Additional notes on Conus aurantius. Haw. Shell News 17 (10), p. 5.

—, 1971. Musical notes. Haw. Shell News 19 (4), p. 4.

—, 1974. Cassidae of the Netherlands Antilles. Haw. Shell News 22 (5), p. 1, 4.

PILSBRY, H. A., 1903. Landshells of Curaçao. Nautilus 17, p. 48.

PILSBRY, H. A. & B. SHARP, 1897. Scaphopoda. Manual Conch. 17 (1), 348 p.

REGTEREN ALTENA, C. O. VAN, 1941. Old tertiary Mollusca from Curaçao. Proc. Ned. Akad. Wet., Ser.B, 44, p. 1234-1238.

—, 1961. The Mollusca from the limestone of Brimstone Hill, St. Kitts, and Sugar Loaf and White Wall, St. Eustatius, Lesser Antilles. Proc. Kon. Ned. Akad. Wet., ser.B, 64, p. 288-304.

RIGHI, G., 1968. On the radulae and spines of some Polyplacophora and Archaeogastropoda from Curaçao. Stud. Fauna Curaçao 25, p. 58-75.

SCHEPMAN, M. M., 1915. Mollusca. In: Encycl. Ned. West-Indië 1914-1917, p. 477-482.

SCHRAMM, A., 1867. Cataloque des coquilles et des crustacés de la Guadeloupe envoyés à l'exposition universelle. Basse Terre, 27 p.

SIMONS, G. J., 1868. Beschrijving van het eiland Curaçao. Oosterwolde, 156 p.

SMITH, E. A., 1898. On the land-shells of Curaçao and the neighbouring islands. Proc. Malac. Soc. 3, p. 113-116.

SNELLEN VAN VOLLENHOVEN, P. C. T., 1875. Drie nieuwe Choreutinen. Tijdschr. Entomol. 18, p. 70-78.

SYPKENS SMIT, M. P. & A. H. VERSTEEG, 1988. An archaeological reconaissance of St. Martin. In: Stud. honour P. Wagenaar Hummelinck. Amsterdam, p. 261-291.

TEENSTRA, M. D., 1836-1837. De Nederlandsche West-Indische eilanden in derzelver tegenwoordige toestand. Amsterdam, 2 vols.

VANATTA, E. G., 1901. New marine mollusks. Proc. Acad. nat. Sci. Philad. 53, p. 182-188.

VENMANS, L. A. W. C., 1963. Caribbean land molluscs: Streptaxidae. Stud. Fauna Curaçao 14, p. 41-76.

VERNHOUT, J. M., 1914. The land- and freshwater Molluscs of the Dutch West-Indian islands. Notes Leyden Mus. 36, p. 177-189.

VINK, D., 1974. A strange food preference of Conus aurantius. Haw. Shell News 22 (12), p. 8.

VRIES, W. DE, 1974. Caribbean land molluscs: notes on Cerionidae. Stud. Fauna Curaçao 45, p. 81-118.

WAGENAAR HUMMELINCK, P., 1940. Studies on the fauna of Curaçao, Aruba, Bonaire and the Venezuelan islands. Utrecht, 130 p. (Thesis Univ. Utrecht.)

—, 1940. Mollusks of the genera Cerion and Tudora. Stud. Fauna Curaçao 2, p. 43-83.

—, 1963. Curaçaose malacologische problemen. Corr. blad Ned. Malac. Ver. 102, p. 1056-1063.

WULP, F. M. VAN DER, 1882. Remarks on certain American Diptera in the Leiden Museum and description of nine new species. Notes Leyden Mus. 4, p. 73-92.

INDEX OF SHELLS AND PERSONAL NAMES

Americardia antillarum, 174
Americardia guppyi, 174
Anslijn, N., 19
Aspella anceps, 90
Australorbis, 23
Backhuys, Willem, 18, 26
Baker, H. Burrington, 20
Baly, Camille, 16, 192
Bavay, Arthur, 29
Beadle, Elias Root, 24, 30
Berthella quadridens, 152
Bland, Thomas, 26, 27, 30
Bursa crassa, 86
Bursa cubania, 86
Bursa granularis, 86
Bursa livida, 88
Bursa ponderosa, 88
Bursa rhodostoma, 88
Bursa spadicea, 86
Bursa thomae, 88
Cadulus dominguensis, 182
Caecum, 40
Caecum rijgersmai, 35
Cardium angulatum, 168
Cardium bullatum, 170
Cardium glabratum, 172
Cardium graniferum, 174
Cardium petitianum, 170
Cardium ringiculum, 170
Cardium rugosum, 168
Cardium senticosum, 166
Cardium serratum, 172
Cardium subelongatum, 168
Carpenter, P. P., 28, 54, 66, 92, 174
Cassis abbreviata, 74
Cassis flammea, 70, 72
Cassis granulosa, 74
Cassis inflata, 74, 76
Cassis madagascariensis, 68
Cassis recurvirostris, 76
Cassis tessalatum, 74
Cassis tuberosa, 70, 72
Cassis ventricosa, 74
Cerion uva, 20
Cerodrilla coccinata, 150

Charonia tritonis, 114
Charonia variegata, 114
Cistulops raveni, 20
Colbeau, Jules A. J., 14, 32
Colubraria lanceolata, 120
Colubraria obscura, 118
Colubraria testacea, 118
Conus arausiacus, 132
Conus armillatus, 146
Conus aurantius, 124
Conus aureofasciatus, 138
Conus barbadensis, 126
Conus caracteristicus, 136
Conus cardinalis, 128
Conus cedonulli, 122
Conus centurio, 130
Conus clerii, 136
Conus coffeae, 132
Conus columba, 134
Conus cretaceus, 130
Conus daucus, 132
Conus duvallii, 130
Conus echinulatus, 130
Conus ermineus, 142
Conus fumigatus, 132
Conus granulatus, 144
Conus jaspideus, 130
Conus leoninus, 138
Conus leucostictus, 124
Conus magellanicus, 124
Conus mazei, 146
Conus mercator, 144
Conus mindanus, 130
Conus minutus, 136
Conus mus, 126
Conus muscosus, 136
Conus narcissus, 142
Conus nebulosus, 122
Conus ochraceus, 140
Conus portoricanus, 142
Conus proteus, 140
Conus puncticulatus, 134
Conus pusio, 134
Conus pygmaeus, 134
Conus questor, 136

Conus regius, 122
Conus reticulatus, 144
Conus roseus, 128
Conus speciosissimus, 124
Conus spurius, 138, 140
Conus testudinarius, 142
Conus transiensis, 132
Conus tribunus, 130
Conus verrucosus, 130
Cope, Edward Drinker, 13, 28, 30
Crassispira affinis, 148
Crassispira cancellata, 148
Cymatium americanum, 98
Cymatium antillarum, 98
Cymatium aquatilis, 100
Cymatium caribbaeum, 106
Cymatium chlorostomum, 102
Cymatium costatum, 98
Cymatium cynocephalum, 106
Cymatium femorale, 96
Cymatium fusiformis, 108
Cymatium gibbosum, 112
Cymatium gracilis, 104
Cymatium krebsii, 108
Cymatium labiosum, 110
Cymatium loroisii, 110
Cymatium martinianum, 100
Cymatium muricinum, 98
Cymatium nicobaricum, 102
Cymatium olearium, 98, 100
Cymatium parthenopeum, 98
Cymatium pileare, 100
Cymatium rutilum, 110
Cymatium tuberosum, 98
Cymatium vespaceum, 104
Cyphoma gibbosa, 92
Cypraea acicularis, 58
Cypraea aubreyana, 58
Cypraea bicallosa, 58
Cypraea bifasciata, 54
Cypraea cervinetta, 54
Cypraea cervus, 52
Cypraea cinerea, 56
Cypraea dubia, 54
Cypraea exanthema, 54
Cypraea flaveola, 58
Cypraea helvola, 52
Cypraea mus, 60
Cypraea plumbea, 54

Cypraea sordida, 56
Cypraea spurca, 58
Cypraea succincta, 56
Cypraea surinamensis, 58
Cypraea translucens, 56
Cypraea zebra, 54
Cypraecassis testiculus, 78
Damon, Robert, 26, 32
Daphnella candidula, 151
Daphnella clathrata, 151
Delden, R. O. van, 16
Dentalium antillarum, 180
Dentalium disparile, 182
Dentalium semistriatum, 180
Dentalium translucidum, 180
Detracia bullaoides, 160
Distorsio clathratus, 114
Dolabrifera ascifera, 154
Dolium, 68, 82, 84
Emarginula, 40
Epidromus, 118
Epitonium, 32
Eupera viridante, 22
Fock van Coppenaal, Gerrit M. D., 29
Gastrocopta curacoana, 20
Gill, Theodore, 92
Greiner, A., 2
Gräfing, M. H. van Rijgersma, 10, 11, 17
Haliburton, R. G., 31
Harting, Pieter, 12, 25, 31
Heinrici, 13
Hemicardia media, 176
Holthuis, L. B., 9, 31, 192
Horst, C. J. van der, 20, 22
Jentink, F. A., 26
Johnson, W. H. N., 17, 35
Johnson-Waymouth, Ada S. M., 10, 17
Karel XV, King, 13
Kohlmann, Joseph, 12, 25, 29, 35
Krebs, Hendrik Johannes, 19, 32, 98
Laevicardium laevigatum, 172
Mactier, William Laurence, 30
Marie, Edouard-Auguste, 29, 33
Martin, K., 22
Mazé, Hippolyte Pierre, 25, 29, 146
Melampus cingulatus, 160
Melampus coffeus, 156
Melampus flavus, 156
Melampus pusillus, 158

Microceramus bonairensis, 20
Mörch, Otto A. L., 32, 104, 108
Morum dennisoni, 80
Morum lamarckii, 80
Morum oniscus, 80
Muskus, R., 20
Neosimnia acicularis, 94
Neosimnia antillarum, 94
Neosimnia subrostrata, 94
Neosimnia uniplicata, 94
Oniscia, 80
Ovula, 92, 94
Pachybathron, 21, 78
Papyridea hiatus, 170
Papyridea semisulcata, 170
Pedipes mirabilis, 162
Pedipes quadridens, 162
Peeters-Willems, Ineke, 15
Persona, 114
Phalium cicatricosum, 74, 76
Phalium granulatum, 74
Pira monile, 156
Pleurobranchus quadridens, 152
Pleurotoma, 148, 150, 151
Ranella, 86, 88, 112
Ranella hastula, 90
Rawson, R. W., 26, 30, 33, 40, 46, 58, 78, 98, 108
Reed-Waymouth, Henrietta E., 10, 17
Richardson, R. R. H., 16, 192
Rijgersma, Ada H. H. van, 10, 12, 17
Rijgersma, Anna E. M. P. van, 10, 12
Rijgersma, Cornelis W. van, 10, 14
Rijgersma, Eling Hendriks van, 10, 11
Rijgersma, Hendrik Fling van, 10, 11, 14
Rijgersma, Henricus Eling van, 10, 11
Rijgersma, Marie Catharina van, 10, 11
Rijgersma, S. Gardengius van, 10, 14, 17, 35
Rijgersma, S. Gardingius van, 10, 13
Rijgersma, Trijntje de Tempe van, 10, 13
Rijgersma-Lang, Helen van, 10, 17, 27
Schramm, Alphonse, 29
Sharp, B., 21
Snellen van Vollenhoven, S., 9, 12, 31
Sowerby, George B., 26, 32, 102
Stolk, T. van, 12
Strombus accipitrinus, 44, 46
Strombus bituberculatus, 50
Strombus costatus, 44, 46
Strombus dubius, 44
Strombus gallus, 42, 50
Strombus gigas, 23, 38, 40
Strombus goliath, 38
Strombus gracilior, 48
Strombus granulatus, 38
Strombus inermis, 46
Strombus lentiginosus, 38
Strombus lobatus, 42, 50
Strombus pugilis, 38, 48
Strombus raninus, 50
Suringar, W. F. R., 26
Swift, R., 13, 25, 27, 30, 33, 98, 118
Tenaturris angulifera, 150
Tonna galea antillarum, 84
Tonna maculosa, 82
Tonna perdix, 82, 84
Tonna perdix occidentalis, 82
Trachycardium isocardia, 164, 168
Trachycardium magnum, 168
Trachycardium muricatum, 166, 168
Tralia ovula, 158
Trigonulina ornata, 176, 178
Triton, 40, 96, 114, 116, 118
Trivia antillarum, 66
Trivia armandina, 62
Trivia cimex, 64
Trivia coccinella, 64
Trivia globosa, 66
Trivia labiosa, 64
Trivia leucosphaera, 66
Trivia nivea, 64
Trivia nix, 64
Trivia pediculus, 64
Trivia pilula, 66
Trivia quadripunctata, 62
Trivia rotunda, 62
Trivia subrostrata, 66
Trivia suffusa, 62
Trivia sulcata, 64
Truncatella, 162
Tudora muskusi, 20
Ulricht, B., 13
Verticordia ornata, 178
Volva, 94
Waymouth, Josiah Charles, 10, 17
Willis, John Robert, 31
Zaagman, Jurrien, 4, 34, 36, 192

ACKNOWLEDGEMENTS

With the publication of the second book about doctor Van Rijgersma's watercolours and manuscripts, the author would like to express thanks to his colleagues of the Zoological Museum in Amsterdam: director Drs Wouter Los for his stimulating attention, collection manager Robert G. Moolenbeek for help and advise, Pit Rincker and Carolien Boerma for typework and preparing the index, Jurrien Zaagman and Louis van der Laan for drawings and photographs.

On Curaçao Governor Dr. René A. Römer always shows interest in cultural work and scientific research, and so does Minister Edsel A. V. Jesurun at The Hague. The OKSNA, secretary-general Ifna Isenia, kindly supplied funds for this book which was, like the 'Flowers from St. Martin', excellently published by the Walburg Pers through the skillful hands of Johan van 't Leven and John Smal.

At St. Martin Lt. Governor Mr. Ing. R. R. H. Richardson and President of the Council of the Arts, Camille Baly, were superb hosts and helpful in the historic research of the island.

My admiration to Dr. L. B. Holthuis who discovered doctor H. E. van Rijgersma 33 years ago.

Finally my wife Maritza Coomans-Eustatia, because she gave the idea to publish both manuscripts in colour, supplied the antique maps on the fly-leaves, and helped in many ways.

Dr. Henry E. Coomans
  Chairman Dept. Malacology
  Institute of Taxonomic Zoology
  (Zoological Museum)
  University of Amsterdam

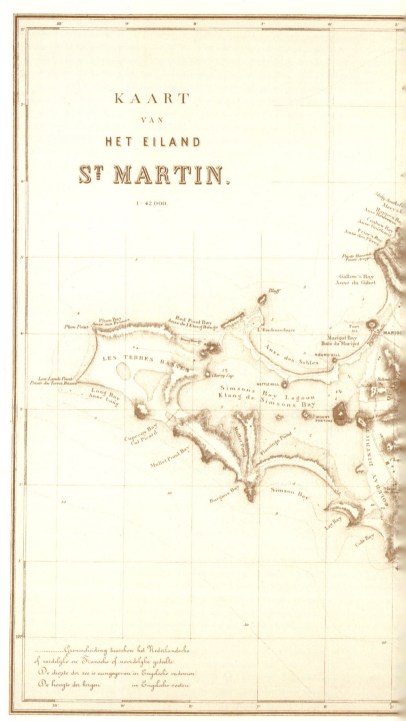

Map of 'The island St. Martin'. I. Dornseiffen, 1883.